Criminal Justice
Recent Scholarship

Edited by
Marilyn McShane and Frank P. Williams III

A Series from LFB Scholarly

Social Structure-Social Learning and Delinquency
Mediation or Moderation?

Stephen W. Verrill

LFB Scholarly Publishing LLC
New York 2008

Library of Congress Cataloging-in-Publication Data

Verrill, Stephen W., 1963-
  Social structure-social learning and delinquency : mediation or moderation? / Stephen W. Verrill.
      p. cm. -- (Criminal justice : recent scholarship)
  Includes bibliographical references and index.
  ISBN 978-1-59332-241-0 (alk. paper)
  1. Social learning. 2. Social structure. 3. Criminal behavior,
Prediction of. 4. Juvenile delinquency. 5. Juvenile delinquents--
Family relationships. 6. Deviant behavior. 7. Parent and child--
Psychological aspects. I. Title.
  HQ783.V47 2008
  305.23086'92--dc22

2007050638

ISBN 978-1-59332-241-0

Printed on acid-free 250-year-life paper.

Manufactured in the United States of America.

Table of Contents

Acknowledgements

I thank Chris Sellers for providing the micro-level data used in these analyses, as well as Jennifer Wareham for the addition of the macro-level data. I enthusiastically acknowledge academic debts to forensic psychologist Duane Dobbert, criminologists Chris Sellers, John Cochran, and Tom Winfree, and political scientist Diane Verrill. Lastly, I thank Leo Balk for making this book happen.

CHAPTER 1

Social Learning Theory

INTRODUCTION

Overview

Social learning theory (Akers, 1973, 1977, 1985, 1998; Burgess & Akers, 1966) is an established general theory of criminal, deviant, and conforming behavior that integrates operant conditioning with cognitively oriented psychological and sociological theories, notably Sutherland's (1947) differential association theory. Social learning theory is a general theory that describes the learning process involved in an individual's history and opportunity for crime (Akers, 1998).

Social learning theory has received much empirical attention, and its concepts and variables find moderate to strong support with survey, official, cross-sectional, and longitudinal data (e.g., Akers & Lee, 1996; Akers, Krohn, Lanza-Kaduce & Radosevich, 1979; Conway & McCord, 2002; Haynie, 2002; V. Johnson, 1988; Winfree, Mays & Backstrom, 1994). When researchers employ theory competition, social learning theory concepts and propositions generally find more support than those derived from other simultaneously tested theories (e.g., Akers & Cochran, 1985; Alarid, Burton & Cullen, 2000; Benda, 1994; Kandel & Davies, 1991; Burton, Cullen, Evans & Dunaway, 1994; Hinduja, 2006; Matsueda & Heimer, 1987; Neff & Waite, 2007; Rebellon, 2002; White, Johnson & Horowitz, 1986). When scholars apply social learning concepts and propositions to integrated theory, social learning variables generally have the strongest effect (e.g., Conger, 1976; Elliott, Huizinga & Ageton, 1985; R. Johnson, Marcos

& Bahr, 1987; Marcos, Bahr & Johnson, 1986; Thornberry, Lizotte, Krohn, Farnworth & Jang, 1994; White, Pandina & LaGrange, 1987).

Despite the large body of research, there is still much unknown about the social learning process, and scholars continually seek to test social learning theory's scope. Much of the social learning body of science involves explaining minor forms of juvenile offending and substance use (Akers et al., 1979; Krohn, Skinner, Massey & Akers, 1985; Winfree & Bernat, 1998). One direction recent research has taken has been to examine broader offenses and populations of offenders. For example, social learning variables partially accounted for illegal computer behavior (W.F. Skinner & Fream, 1997) intimate partner violence (Sellers, Cochran & Winfree, 2003), and digital piracy (Higgins, Fell, & Wilson, 2006) in samples of college students. Parents and peers were found to influence adolescent drug use in Korea (Hwang & Akers, 2006). The theory has further found support in explaining deviance in police officers (Chappell & Piquero, 2004), drinking behavior in people 60 years old or older (Akers, La Greca, Cochran & Sellers, 1989), marijuana use in rural middle school students (Winfree & Griffiths, 1983), and alcohol and drug use in American Indian youths (Winfree, Griffiths & Sellers, 1989).

The vast body of research on social learning theory has demonstrated that individual deviant behavior varies depending on the individual's associations, definitions, reinforcements, and to some extent, imitation of deviant models. The theory appears to identify with a fair degree of accuracy the basic mechanism by which individuals learn deviant behavior. As satisfactory as the theory might be, though, it still has limitations.

In its strictly social psychological (processual) form, social learning cannot answer why some individuals and not others encounter configurations of the social learning elements conducive to deviant behavior. Such a solution requires the integration of macro-sociological (structural) concepts into social learning theory. Akers (1998) has proposed such an integration, terming the social learning elaboration "social structure-social learning."

In this latest explication of the theory, Akers (1998) suggests that social learning theory mediates social structural influences on individual criminal behavior and ultimately on crime rates. Akers postulates that social structure acts as the distal cause of crime, affecting an individual's exposure to norm and norm-violating contingencies. The social learning variables differential association, definitions, imitation, and differential reinforcement, and other discriminative stimuli, mediate social structure's effect on individual behavior, providing the proximate causes of crime. Much like social learning theory is derived from Sutherland's (1947) theory of differential association, social structure-social learning also has roots in Sutherland's work.

Sutherland (1939) began with an interest in explaining both crime and criminal behavior, which led to a theory that discussed both macrosocial and microsocial structures and processes. Sutherland (1947) revised the theory, however, such that its final version constrained itself to microsocial processes. What began as a broad, general theory of both crime and criminal behavior ended up as a delimited explanation of the general processes that influence deviant and conforming behavior at the individual level of explanation.

Sutherland (1947) retained the notion that social disorganization and normative conflict are involved in the formation of individual criminal behavior, that differential social organization provides the opportunity for differential associations to occur, but his final version of the theory did not specify the links between social structure and criminal behavior. Sutherland remained interested in both an epidemiological and etiological explanation for crime and criminal behavior, but his formal theoretical statements excluded macrosocial considerations.

Burgess and Akers (1966) revised Sutherland's processual theory to better specify the learning process, keeping the theory focused on the microsocial level. Akers (1998) later elaborated social learning theory such that it attempts to explain both the macrosocial structure and microsocial processes that lead to deviant or conforming behavior, and ultimately crime rates, by viewing social structure as the learning environment for individual behavior (Akers, 1968). Akers (1998) revisited the formal cross-level specification of crime causality abandoned by Sutherland (1939, 1947).

Akers (1998) referenced Sutherland's (1947) earlier lack of macrosocial linking propositions as an impetus for his explicating social structure-social learning theory. Although Sampson (1999) and Krohn (1999) have suggested that Akers (1998) likewise fails to provide suitable linking propositions between social structure and social learning, Akers (1999) suggests that the model suitably specifies the relationships such that it is ready for empirical testing.

Although acknowledging the concerns about macrosocial variables, Akers (1999) concludes that social structure-social learning theory requires better empirical testing with cross-level data, not further theorizing. Akers (1998) and colleagues (Lee et al., 2004) suggest that research in this area should test more comprehensive models that include broader indicators of social structure, especially those derived from macrosocial theories of crime.

The point of the social structure-social learning specification is that social structure only influences individual behavior through its influence on social learning variables. The theory hypothesizes that theoretical concepts already known to influence crime rates do so through their influence on reinforcement contingencies. Therefore, the social structure-social learning model does account for theoretically derived macrosocial determinants.

Although a comprehensive explanation of crime and criminal behavior addresses both individual differences in crime formation and the structure that shapes the process (Akers, 1968; Shaw, Zorbaugh, McKay & Cottrell, 1929), there are barriers to testing such a model. Notably, data allowing for the simultaneous examination of macrosocial and microsocial variables are uncommon (Lanza-Kaduce & Capece, 2003). Despite these hindrances, there are four direct tests of the social structure-social learning elaboration in the literature (Bellair et al., 2003; Lanza-Kaduce & Capece, 2003; Lanza-Kaduce, Capece, & Alden, 2006; Lee et al., 2004; see also Hoffmann, 2002).

In one study with limited structural measures, researchers concluded that family well being and social learning partially mediated the impact of occupational structure on adolescent violence (Bellair et al., 2003). In another study, researchers concluded that social learning partially mediated the relationship between structural variables and binge drinking (Lanza-Kaduce & Capece, 2003). Lanza-Kaduce and colleagues (2006) later reported that in a study with limited structural variables, as well as limited social learning variables (risks and rewards only), social structure-social learning concepts received very little, if any, support in the context of feminist theory applied to college student deviant behavior, as opposed to necessarily criminal behavior (Lanza-Kaduce et al., 2006). Finally, researchers concluded that social learning partially mediated the relationship between structural variables and adolescent substance use (Lee et al., 2004). Although measured imperfectly, and utilizing varying and limited statistical techniques, three studies report findings that are suggestive that social learning variables mediate structural influences on individual behavior.

Aims of this Book

As the tests in the literature have not incorporated strong social structural measures, Akers (1998, 1999) and colleagues (Lee et al., 2004) suggest that research on the social structure-social learning model should test models that include broader indicators of social structure, especially theoretically derived measures. It is this suggestion on which this research focuses.

This book contributes to the theoretical body of literature through its more complete measurement of the macrosocial correlates and theoretically defined structural causes dimensions. Notably, the present research measures race, poverty, and family disruption, three variables that Pratt and Cullen (2005) identified in a macro-level predictors meta-analysis as "among the strongest and most stable predictors " (p. 373) of crime, and which some researchers think of as indicators of a "concentrated disadvantage" construct (e.g., Sampson & Raudenbush, 1999; Sampson, Raudenbush & Earls, 1997). Further, this book measures social disorganization theory variables in a manner similar to that used by Sampson (Sampson & Groves, 1989), one of the social structure-social learning model's more vocal skeptics (Sampson, 1999). Secondly, this book introduces possible linkages between social structure and the social learning process in an attempt to address the concerns of Krohn (1999), who suggested that the theory does not adequately do so, and Sampson (1999), who suggested that the theory is incapable of producing a priori, refutable macrosocial propositions.

This book also critically examines Akers' (1998) notion that social learning mediates the relationship between social structure and crime, introducing the possibility that social learning may instead moderate social structure's effect on crime and criminal behavior. The argument in this book does not dismiss social structure-social learning out of hand and insist on a moderating relationship from the start, along with its inherent methods of testing community factors (e.g., HLM), as do some oppositional theorists, nor does it automatically accept on its face the social structure and social learning relationships and related conclusions described by Akers and colleagues. Instead, this book's argument starts with Akers' theory, examines the theory with data suitable to both community-level and microsocial testing, using methodology specifically aimed at examining Akers' mediation hypotheses. This book presents an argument suggesting that clarifying the distinction of mediation or moderation may contribute to understanding how exactly social structure might influence the social learning process. These are weighty tasks, and there is much work to be done, but combined, the two aims of this book, utilizing more complete social structural measures and explaining how social structure might impinge on the social learning process, respond to Akers' (1999) plea to help specify the most underdeveloped portion of the model. This book offers new dialogue toward that end.

CHAPTER 2

Social Structure-Social Learning

DIFFERENTIAL ASSOCIATION

In order to understand the complexity of the social learning model, as well as its social structural elaboration, it is first necessary to trace its historical development, beginning with the inception of Sutherland's (1939, 1947) differential association theory. Sutherland (1939) sought a general theory of crime that would resolve failings in the literature, advance criminology as a science, and provide for the meaningful control of crime (Sutherland, 1924).

Sutherland (1939) believed that prevailing theories of criminal behavior were inadequate to provide meaningful understanding and control, resulting instead in a scattered body of knowledge that provided little practical application. One approach, for example, viewed crime as a product of a variety of individual factors. As individual criminal behavior derived from these situationally different factors, the approach did not allow for general explanations that would hold without exception (see historical discussions in Matsueda, 1988; Sutherland & Cressey, 1970). Sutherland (1939, 1973a) was concerned that such a multiple-factor approach was not scientific, resulting in unsound theorizing.

Sutherland (1939) instead favored general statements of criminal behavior that would aid in both the understanding and control of crime. Rather than view crime as the particularistic product of numerous factors (Sutherland & Cressey, 1974), Sutherland (1939) sought a set of universal statements. He believed that an organized, scientific theory of criminal behavior, however tentative, was necessary to bring discussion and understanding to bear on issues that would otherwise go unsolved if not advanced until theoretically complete. Sutherland considered his theory tentative and hypothetical, needing future examination against data, but necessary to start a discussion based on science.

Building off his sociological training and notion that a theory of criminal behavior should center on learning, interaction, and communication, Sutherland (1973a) sought an account of all crime causation facts. He wished to express general statements that accounted for all known correlates of criminal behavior, without exception, from a sociological viewpoint.

In formulating his theory, Sutherland (1939) followed three guidelines. First, comprehensive criminological theory must acknowledge and consider all reasonable explanations for criminal behavior. Sutherland classified existing explanations for crime into two groups: individual and situational or cultural.

Sutherland (1939) suggested that individual explanations emphasized inherited or acquired traits, such as feeblemindedness and anatomical or emotional deviations. Individual explanations were concerned with the differences of people, viewing criminal behavior as derived from individual defects (see Sutherland, 1973b) and considering such personal abnormalities as the primary cause of crime (see Sutherland, 1973c).

The situational or cultural difference perspective emphasized social processes. Sutherland (1939) characterized these processes as occurring either at the small group level, such as families and neighborhoods, at the institutional level, reflected in economic and political systems, or more generally in the form of differential associations, cultural conflicts, and societal social disorganization. Situational and cultural difference viewpoints considered crime as part of a process (see Sutherland, 1924).

Sutherland's second theory-construction guideline hinged on the notion of desire. Sutherland (1939) suggested that crime involved more mechanisms than offender needs and restraints, and that many theories focused too narrowly on desire and inhibition. He believed that a general theory of criminal behavior must additionally account for more elements, such as results, external restraints, public opinion, possibility of detection and punishment, technical ability, and other related factors (see Sutherland, 1939).

Third, Sutherland (1939) acknowledged the multiple-factor viewpoint that criminal behavior is sometimes adventitious, but he reasoned that criminal behavior is only beyond analytic possibility at the complex, individual circumstances level. He equated that notion with the chance inherent in a coin flip coming up heads or tails. Sutherland reasoned that the coin's outcome, similar to behavior involving individual circumstances, is not without cause but that the cause is too complicated to distinguish at the level of occurrence. He carried the analogy further, suggesting that unlike the two limited outcomes of a coin toss, and instead like the roll of loaded dice, individually circumstanced behavior involves numerous outcomes, some of which although not certain, are more probable than other behaviors. Sutherland concluded that a general theory of crime must focus on systematic criminal behavior, rather than adventitious, individually circumstanced behavior, in order to discover general and uniform processes (see Sutherland, 1939).

Methodologically, Sutherland (1939) embraced Lindesmith's (1938) application of analytic induction to test for necessary and sufficient causes. The approach specified a case-by-case search for exceptions to a hypothesis and upon finding one, necessitated either a modification of the hypothesis or a redefinition of the universe of cases. The idea was that after investigating a number of segments of criminality and finding no exception, the series of general propositions about those segments would lead, with *practical certainty*, to a general body of criminological theory (Sutherland, 1939).

Sutherland (1939) dealt with the problematic issue of multiple causal factors that differ individually by abstracting individual criminal behavior to systematic criminal behavior. Sutherland was vague on the term's meaning, but as he used *adventitious* and *systematic* to distinguish opposing viewpoints, it is likely that Sutherland defined adventitious criminal behavior as sporadic and multi-sourced, contrasted with systematic criminal behavior as planned and regular (see Sutherland, 1973a).

Sutherland (1939) intended systematic criminal behavior to serve as the framework for the formulation of scientific statements about individual behavior. He acknowledged criminal behavior as adventitious when considered from the point of view of individual circumstances, but as he sought universal statements, he abstracted the behavior under study in order to avoid the consideration of trivial crimes with immeasurable causes. Sutherland evaded the question of multiple crime causes, adventitious crime, by defining crime in a way that emphasized behavioral commonalities and ignored individually specific factors that he viewed as rare (see Sutherland, 1973a).

Believing it impossible to account for all situations that might lead a specific individual to commit a specific crime, Sutherland (1939) reasoned that a theory that explained systematic criminal behavior would accordingly explain specific acts generally. He used organized criminal behavior and criminal careers as examples of systematic criminal behavior, and he believed that *practically all criminals* would fall into the category (Sutherland, 1973a). Sutherland created the concept of systematic criminal behavior as a matter of convenience (see Sutherland, 1973a), perhaps redefining the universe up front so that he would not have to modify the hypotheses based on trivial, incidental exceptions.

In the first statement of his theory, Sutherland (1939) organized scientific characteristics of crime into a general explanation that addressed both the epidemiology and etiology of crime and criminal behavior. His seven general statements refer to systematic criminal behavior, a concept he created to allow for the formulation of universal statements about criminal behavior (propositions one, two, three, four, and five) and crime rates (propositions six and seven). Sutherland was interested in the causes of criminal behavior generally, the gross facts regarding crime (Cressey, 1960), as he believed that incidental crime, although causally similar to systematic criminal behavior, would contain exceptional cases due to its adventitious character (Sutherland, 1939, 1973b).

Sutherland's (1939) seven general statements refer to systematic criminal behavior, a concept he created to allow for the formulation of universal statements about criminal behavior (propositions one, two, three, four, and five) and crime rates (propositions six and seven). Sutherland was interested in the causes of criminal behavior generally, the gross facts regarding crime (Cressey, 1960), as he believed that incidental crime, although causally similar to systematic criminal behavior, would contain exceptional cases due to its adventitious character (Sutherland, 1939, 1973b).

Regardless of the conceptual unit of analysis, Sutherland's (1939) ideas represented a formal organization of his earlier approaches to the subject, inherent in the hypotheses,

> First, any person can be trained to adopt and follow any pattern of behavior which he is able to execute. Second, failure to follow a prescribed pattern of behavior is due to the

inconsistencies and lack of harmony in the influences which direct the individual. Third, the conflict of culture is therefore the fundamental principle in the explanation of crime. (Sutherland, 1934, pp. 51-52)

Sutherland (1939) suggested that both lawful and unlawful behavior developed from differing messages gained during the process of associating with others. Etiologically, Sutherland identified differential association, association with people who engage in systematic criminal behavior, as the proximate cause of systematic criminal behavior.

Sutherland (1924) reasoned that at birth, individuals are born with both innate physiological tendencies and general tendencies that vary by social conditions. Sutherland posited that *human nature* comprised both individual and group phenomena. Focusing on general tendencies, he argued that intellectual expressions, anger, sympathy, imitation, and the like derive from contacts with others. Although physiological tendencies such as sneezing and frowning are innate, and may occur in complete isolation from others, general tendencies are general expressions of social events that only derive from social interaction (see Sutherland, 1932). Sutherland (1924) maintained that these general expressions would not occur in complete isolation from others, and because social interactions vary, both lawful and unlawful behavior represent expressions of human nature—expressions of varied social interactions that are developed through the same social process (Sutherland, 1932).

Influenced by the epidemiology of the Chicago School, Sutherland (1939) viewed social disorganization as the distal cause of systematic criminal behavior. He argued that historically, society provided uniform and consistent societal influences. As society moved away from small communities, mobility, competition, and conflict resulted in a state of social disorganization. Sutherland marks the colonization of America as a starting point to social disorganization, particularly noting the industrial revolution, capitalism, competition, and democracy as strong factors. He commented,

This sequence of events necessarily resulted in an immense increase in crime. In the first place the large family and the homogeneous neighborhood, which had been the principal agencies of social control, disintegrated, primarily as the result of mobility. They were replaced by the small family, consisting of parents and children, detached from other relatives, and by a neighborhood in which the mores were not homogeneous, and the behavior of one person was a matter of relative indifference to other persons. Thus the agencies by which control had been secured in almost all earlier societies were greatly weakened. (Sutherland, 1939, p. 71)

Sutherland (1939) viewed crime as a social phenomenon comprising three elements: appreciated value by a politically important group; cultural conflict by part of the group, resulting in unappreciated or less appreciated value; and coercion by those who appreciate the value against those who do not appreciate the value. Simply, to Sutherland, crime represented the description of events that occurred when one important group sanctioned mores that were otherwise acceptable behavior to others. Sutherland suggested that all crimes contained this set of relationships when viewed at the group, rather than the individual, level, and he adopted the view that crime was an antagonistic action of an individual against one's group.

Influenced by his work with Sellin (1938), Sutherland (1939) expressed culture conflict as an underlying cause of differential association and therefore a special case of social disorganization. Culture conflict reflects the characterization of the groups creating and punishing the violation of mores, versus the groups not in agreement with the mores. Culture conflict provides the link between individual criminal behavior that stems from differential associations, and crime rates that stem from social disorganization.

Sutherland (1939) considered culture conflict a smaller representation of social disorganization. If not for a societal organization of conflicting cultures, a small part of the larger group disagreeing over mores, individuals would have no opportunity to associate with others holding differing values. Culture conflict enables social disorganization to result in systematic criminal behavior. Sutherland emphasized that crime exists only when the violation of such mores does not result in public condemnation, a consensus from the whole group, suggesting that if society organized itself against systematic crime, criminal behavior could not exist.

Sutherland (1939) intended his theory as a tentative statement on criminal behavior and crime, and he invited criticism. Sutherland (1973a) focused his evaluation of critiques in nine areas: (1) the relationship between differential association, social organization, and culture conflict, (2) the distinction between systematic and adventitious crime; (3) the significance of the term differential; (4) the relationship between differential association theory and Tarde's (1912) theory of imitation; (5) what specifically is learned in association with others; (6) whether non-criminals can invent crime; (7) the origin of crime; (8) the modalities of association with criminal versus non-criminal patterns; and (9) the relationship between personal traits and culture in the genesis of criminal behavior.

Further, Sutherland (1973d) vigorously argued his notion of the best case *against* differential association theory in an originally unpublished paper, honing in on opportunity, intensity of need, crime and alternate behaviors, and methodologies (e.g., sufficient causality). Sutherland (1947) subsequently revised the theory, incorporating his responses to what he believed to be important criticisms, whether acceptance or refutation, in the groundwork section leading up to his formal propositions, the propositions themselves, the commentary immediately following the propositions, and the remainder of his book.

First, Sutherland (1947) focused attention on methods of scientific explanation. He specified that he was searching for necessary and sufficient causes, organized in the form of universal statements that, still consistent with analytic induction, contained no exceptions.

To achieve these universal propositions, Sutherland (1947) noted the desirability of abstracting the multiple factors that operate at the instant of occurrence to their common elements. Such abstract propositions treated criminal behavior as a class of events, emphasizing the interrelations among various patterns of behavior (see Sutherland, 1973d). Sutherland sought the intervening mechanisms (see Matsueda, 1988) that occurred in the genesis of criminal behavior, the history of behavior that was present just before the instance of expressed needs, values, goals, and the like (Sutherland, 1947; Sutherland, 1973d). Sutherland (1947) sought to distinguish criminal from non-criminal behavior (Sutherland & Cressey, 1969), arguing that general needs and values require explanation because both criminal and non-criminal behavior represent an expression of general needs and values.

Sutherland (1947) suggested that it was essential to a universal statement of criminal behavior to reinterpret concrete factors known to correlate with crime, such as race, urbanicity, and offender age, so that their abstract mechanisms became apparent. Sutherland noted that otherwise, a general statement about these correlations would be incorrect because the correlations contain exceptions. For instance, not all African Americans commit crime, not all city dwellers commit crime, nor do all juveniles. Sutherland insisted that knowing about these correlations was important, but that a useful theory, one offering universal statements, must identify the commonalities between the correlates and crime. A useful, universal theory must identify the commonalities present in criminal behavior yet absent in non-criminal behavior (Sutherland & Cressey, 1969). Sutherland (1947) offered abstraction as a tool for this purpose.

Next, Sutherland (1947) differentiated levels of explanation. He delimited the problem under analysis to a small part of the larger problem, removing macrosocial statements from his criminological theory and thus restricting his propositions to the individual level. He was interested in the chronology of the criminological problem, and viewed it desirable to hold constant earlier causal processes in the expression of individual criminal behavior (Sutherland & Cressey, 1969).

Sutherland (1947) dispensed with formally seeking distal universal statements as to why an individual has differential associations, the proximate cause of criminal behavior, instead readdressing that issue elsewhere in the book. Sutherland argued that such restricted causal analysis was necessary in order to find valid generalizations. He sought a simple, temporal statement that distinguished criminal behavior from non-criminal behavior, suggesting that it made no difference in the quest for valid generalizations—the derivation of universal statements—how the behaviors themselves came to be.

After specifying the methodology, Sutherland (1947) described two potential research avenues for explaining criminal behavior: explain the instant causes of criminal behavior, the processes operating at the moment of crime (Sutherland & Cressey, 1969), or explain the processes working in the earlier history of criminal behavior. Sutherland referred to the instant causes approach as mechanistic, situational, or dynamic (Sutherland and Cressey, 1969), and he dismissed the approach as falsely separating the individual from the situation, falsely separating the individual from life experiences that define certain situations as opportunities for law breaking (Sutherland, 1947; Sutherland & Cressey, 1969). Conceding that a situational explanation would be superior to other explanations if achievable in a useful manner, Sutherland (1947) considered instant causes the particularistic product of multiple factors. He believed it impossible to isolate and derive universal statements from such personal and social pathologies.

Sutherland (1947) instead favored the earlier history approach, labeling it genetic or historical. The genetic approach examined the processes working in the earlier history of criminal behavior, identifying criminological antecedents in the genesis of criminal behavior (Sutherland, 1973a). Drawing on symbolic interactionism (Mead, 1934; see Dewey, 1931) and his work on criminal life histories (Sutherland, 1937), Sutherland (1947) held that the individual's life experience is important to engagement or not in crime. Sutherland's revised statement of differential association theory is concerned with explaining criminal behavior from the perspective of the individuals engaging in the behavior, maintaining that criminal acts occur when individuals define presented situations as appropriate for the criminal act.

In his earlier statement of the theory, Sutherland (1939) created the term systematic criminal behavior in order to ignore instant processes that he believed to be rare and incidental. He argued that had he looked at behavior generally, rather than systematic behavior, trivial exceptions would have prevented the derivation of universal statements (see Sutherland, 1973a). In the revision, Sutherland (1947) tackled the issue of multiple factors in individual criminal behavior in a way that allowed him to eliminate systematic criminal behavior as a proxy for that behavior.

Sutherland (1973a) realized that he was unclear in his original statement and that critics misunderstood the term systematic criminal behavior. Moreover, he found that researchers had difficulty distinguishing systematic criminal behavior from adventitious criminal behavior. Sutherland (1947) still viewed abstraction as the solution to making universal statements about behavior with multiple causes at the instant of occurrence, but in the revision, he abstracted these multiple factors to their commonalities without labeling such phenomena systematic. Sutherland used the same argument, elaborating a bit on the rationale, but he abandoned the term systematic. As he had originally used the term out of convenience, and realizing that that it no longer held utility (see Sutherland, 1973a), for few understood what he meant, Sutherland (1947) advanced his theory revision as pertaining to all crime.

In his final statement of differential association, Sutherland's (1947) nine statements combine to form a general explanation of the individual formation of criminal behavior. Differential association theory offers a broad explanation of criminal behavior by advancing universal crime causes that exist regardless of earlier social or instant individual conditions (Sutherland & Cressey, 1970; Matsueda, 1988).

Sutherland (1947) discounted typological (proposition one) and micro strain implications of anomie theory (proposition nine), instead drawing on the symbols and gestures (language, action, appearance) implied by symbolic interaction (proposition two), and the broad sociological supposition of learned behavior. Sutherland considered proposition six, an excess of criminal definitions, the central statement of the microsocial theory. Differential association theory's primary assertions are that heredity plays no role in crime, and that criminal behavior is learned in differential association with influential groups holding contradictory definitions of law violation.

Although Sutherland (1947) stated that the revision was restricted to the individual level of analysis, he did revisit his earlier exposition of crime rates (Sutherland, 1939) in his commentary immediately following the revised general propositions. Moreover, Sutherland (1947) retained the concept of culture conflict, using it to expound on the proposition five notions of favorable and unfavorable definitions of the legal code as a manifestation of groups holding contradictory definitions of law. Consequently, despite the qualifications on levels of analysis, and in a different form, Sutherland (1947) did implicitly maintain that criminal behavior derives from a set of complex interrelationships between differential associations, culture conflict, and social disorganization (see Sutherland, 1939). Although Sutherland (1947) specified a distinct microsocial explanation for criminal behavior, the theory remained consistent with the macrosocial explanation for crime rates afforded by the idea of social disorganization (see Cressey, 1960; Matsueda, 1988).

Sutherland (1947; 1973a) placed differential associations into the context of what he called "differential social organization" or "differential group organization," his preferred terms for Shaw and McKay's (1942) description of social disorganization. Agreeing with the notion of social disorganization, Sutherland (1973a) thought the term itself reflected a particularistic point of view. He thought the term differential social organization better captured both types of group organization—groups organized for criminal behavior and groups organized against criminal behavior.

Sutherland (1947) suggested that in a uniform organization of people, there is only one behavioral pattern. In groups (communities) with no uniform organization, such as those developed through mobility or culture conflict, crime may occur. Sutherland viewed culture conflict as "the basic principle in the explanation of crime" (Sutherland, 1973a, p. 20). He viewed crime, enabled by culture conflict, as an expression of social disorganization. He viewed differential social organization as an explanation for crime rates (the collective sum of individual crimes) and differential associations as the explanation of individual criminal behavior.

Sutherland (1947) suggested that differential social organization provides the opportunity for differential associations to occur. By removing social structural statements from the explicit propositions of the final version of the theory, however, Sutherland did not formally express the links between social structure and criminal behavior. He continued to suggest that social disorganization and normative conflict (Cressey, 1960; Matsueda, 1988) play a role in the formation of individual criminal behavior, but he abstracted the concepts to the term differential social organization, and he expressed no specific postulates.

Differential association theory is conceptual. Sutherland (1939, 1947) proposed theoretical relationships between sociological concepts, but he did not operationalize or test his propositions—he offered no data, but rather advanced a theory he believed would find support when tested.

Although research supported the major differential association theory theme (Glaser, 1954; Glueck & Glueck, 1950; Short, 1957, 1958; Reiss, 1951; Reiss & Rhodes, 1964; Voss, 1964; see Glaser, 1960), some researchers expressed concerns that the theory oversimplified the process of learned behavior because it did not fully specify the learning mechanisms that affect behavior (Ball, 1957; see Short, 1960; for a thorough discussion of literary and theoretical critiques, see Cressey, 1960; Sutherland & Cressey, 1970, 1974). The theory's propositions combine for a genetic (historical) explanation of the processes that affect engagement in criminal behavior (Sutherland, 1947). Although stressing an individual's definition of situations, the process that allows an individual to view various situations as opportunities for law violation, the theory proposes that criminal behavior involves all of the mechanisms involved in learning other kinds of behavior. However, differential association theory does not identify those mechanisms.

SOCIAL LEARNING

Burgess and Akers (1966) addressed the task of specifying the learning process left implicit by Sutherland (1947). They were influenced by Cressey (1960), who commented,

[Differential association theory criticism] ranges from simple assertions that the learning process is more complex than the theory states or implies, to the idea that the theory does not adequately take into account some specific type of learning process, such as differential identification. Between these two extremes are assertions that the theory is inadequate because it does not allow for a process in which criminality seems to be "independently invented" by the actor. I am one of the dozen authors who have advanced this kind of criticism, and in this day of role theory, reference group theory, and complex learning theory, it would be foolhardy to assert that this type of general criticism is incorrect. But it is one thing to [criticize] the theory for failure to specify the learning process accurately and another to specify which aspects of the learning process should be included and in what way. (pp. 53-54)

Cressey (1960) dismissed research-free criticisms as proposals for research, rather than valid critiques of differential association theory.

Initially called differential association-reinforcement theory (Burgess & Akers, 1966), social learning theory (Akers, 1973, 1977, 1985, 1998) draws from psychological behavioral and social cognitive theories to specify the differential association learning process. Unlike Jeffery (1965), who also tried to operationalize the learning process, Burgess and Akers kept the core of Sutherland's (1947) theory intact. They restated differential association theory statement by statement in behavioral terms in a numbered format that coincided with the nine differential association theory statements (statement one concurrently addressed differential association theory statements one and eight).

Burgess and Akers (1966) argued that Sutherland's (1947) supposition that learning occurs through interaction with others in social environments was compatible with the operant theory notion that environment shapes individual behavior. Burgess and Akers subscribed that if one accepted the notion that differential association theory was essentially a learning theory, and that criminal behavior and non-criminal behavior are learned through the same process, then it was reasonable to incorporate modern learning knowledge into the theory. They further believed that by incorporating previous changes to differential association theory (Cressey, 1953; Hartung, 1965; Jeffrey, 1965; Sykes & Matza, 1957), with their blending of the symbolic interactionist and behaviorist traditions, their reformulation offered a testable general theory of human behavior (Akers, 1998).

Burgess and Akers (1966) suggested that modern learning theory had sufficiently advanced to the point that Sutherland's (1947) implicit mechanisms were specifiable. They emphasized that whereas Sutherland's differential social organization had sufficiently made sense of crime rates through the idea of normative conflict, the explanation offered for the individual level process was less satisfying because, making use of Vold (1958), psychology and social psychology had not previously advanced enough to distinguish such qualitative differences in human behavior. Sociology did not sufficiently understand determining variables at the individual level of analysis (Burgess & Akers, 1966).

Burgess and Akers (1966) offered differential association-reinforcement theory as an explanation for why some persons exposed to normative conflict engage in criminal behavior. They, like Sutherland (1947), viewed their theory revision as consistent with sociologic epidemiological explanations for variation in crime rates. However, differential association-reinforcement theory, like differential association theory, sought an etiological explanation for criminal behavior.

Akers (1973, 1977, 1985) clarified and revised the seminal differential association-reinforcement model and renamed it social learning theory, tweaking the serial propositions along the way. Social learning theory expands differential association theory. It is not a competing explanation. It offers a broader explanation, specifying the learning process and behavioral mechanisms for all types of deviant behavior, but it does not invalidate the core supposition of differential association theory. Empirical support for differential association theory, therefore, supports social learning theory (Akers, 1998).

Social learning theory no longer relies on the serial statements that tied it to classic differential association theory. Instead, the most recent statement describes the social learning process narratively. Akers (1998) postulated,

> The probability that persons will engage in criminal and deviant behavior is increased and the probability of their conforming to the norm is decreased when they differentially associate with others who commit criminal behavior and espouse definitions favorable to it, are relatively more exposed in-person or symbolically to salient criminal/deviant models, define it as desirable or justified in a situation discriminative for the behavior, and have received in the past and anticipate in the current or future situation relatively greater reward than punishment for the behavior. (p. 50)

Social learning theory stresses four concepts. *Differential association* is an elaboration of that presented in differential association theory (Sutherland, 1947), and it provides the social context for the other three concepts (Akers et al., 1979), the context for the mechanisms inherent in the social learning of behavior (Akers & Sellers, 2004). Differential association refers to exposure to the attitudes and behaviors of others. Such exposure may be direct or indirect and verbal or nonverbal (Akers, 1998).

Differential association is mainly a latent construct of interactional (direct associations with the behavior of others) and normative (exposure to patterns of norms and values) dimensions (Akers, 1998). Associations occur in primary and secondary reference groups such as family, peers, school, work, church, and the like. Each reference group contributes to the learning process through association modalities (Akers, 1998; Sutherland, 1947), providing the context for behavior.

Akers (1998) relies on the four modalities of association initially identified by Sutherland: frequency, duration, priority, and intensity (Akers, 1998; Sutherland, 1947). Frequency refers to how often one associates with another, whereas duration identifies the amount of time spent in those associations. Priority time-orders the influence of associations, and intensity estimates their importance (e.g., how close one feels to another).

There is much research on peers and delinquency, with peer association usually measured as the summation of the number or a proportion of friends who engage in delinquent behavior. However, a comprehensive measure of differential association captures more than the single-item measure of the number of deviant friends. The concept involves influential associations broadly to include more groups than friends alone, as well as varied modalities of association (e.g., Akers et al., 1979; Lee et al., 2004). Akers and colleagues (1979) comment,

> [P]rincipal behavioral effects come from interaction in or under the influence of those groups which control individuals' major sources of reinforcement and punishment and expose them to behavioral models and normative definitions. The most important of these groups with which one is in differential association are the peer-friendship groups and the family but they also include schools, churches, and other groups. (p. 638)

The literature reports a consistent correlation between delinquent behavior and delinquent friends (Akers et al., 1979; Brownfield & Thompson, 2002; Elliott et al., 1985; Glueck & Glueck, 1950; Hirschi, 1969; Jaquith, 1981; R. Johnson et al., 1987; Matsueda & Anderson, 1998; Short, 1958; Voss, 1964; Zhang & Messner, 2000). The number of delinquent friends one has is the best external predictor of an individual's criminal behavior (Akers et al., 1979; Elliott et al., 1985; R. Johnson et al., 1987; Warr, 2002). The best external predictor of an adolescent's incidence and amount of drug use is the extent of association with others who use drugs (Elliott et al., 1985; Jaquith, 1981; see also Flom, Friedman, Kottiri, Neaigus & Curtis, 2001; Urberg, 1997). Scholars differ, however, on their interpretation of peer associations.

Some scholars view differential association (Akers, 1998; Sutherland, 1947) as associating with bad companions. The supposition is that "birds of a feather flock together" (Glueck & Glueck, 1950, p. 164). Scholars suggest that delinquents may seek out other delinquents because of common interests (Glueck & Glueck, 1950; M. Gottfredson & Hirschi, 1987; Hirschi, 1969). Besides the social selection effect (Robbins, 1974), they also note that delinquent acts often occur in groups (Erickson & Jensen, 1997; Gold, 1970; see also Warr, 1996, 2002). In such interpretations, the onset of delinquency precedes the onset of exposure to deviant others. Further, some scholars suggest that the relationship between delinquent behavior and delinquent friends may be spurious. Indirect measures of peer delinquency may represent the same construct as self-reported delinquency (M. Gottfredson & Hirschi, 1987; M. Gottfredson & Hirschi, 1990; Kandel, 1996; see also Regnerus, 2002; Urberg, 1992; Zhang & Messner, 2000).

Other scholars view the onset of exposure to deviant friends as occurring before the onset of delinquency (Akers, 1998; Bandura, 1977; Burgess & Akers, 1966; Elliott & Menard, 1996; Sutherland, 1947). Further, some scholars do not view peer delinquency as an artifact of self-reporting measures, but rather view self-reported delinquency and reporting of peer deviancy as distinct measures of delinquency (Flom et al., 2001). Moreover, perceived peer behavior may be as important as actual peer behavior (Iannotti & Busch, 1992).

Social learning theory suggests that the onset of exposure to deviant friends typically occurs before the onset of delinquency (Akers, 1998). However, the theory's reciprocal model does not preclude delinquents from forming associations with other delinquents (Akers & Lee, 1996; Elliott & Menard, 1996; Warr, 2002). Rather, social learning theory predicts (Akers, 1998) and research supports (Farrell & Danish, 1993; Jessor, Jessor & Finney, 1973; Kandel & Davies, 1991; Krohn, Lizotte, Thornberry, Smith & McDowall, 1996; Oetting & Beauvais, 1987; Sellers & Winfree, 1990; Warr, 1993) peers influencing each other mutually (but see discussion in Sampson, 1999).

Social learning theory addresses the causal ordering of peer associations and deviancy through the differential associations concept, and its various modalities of association. The notion of priority (Akers, 1998; Sutherland, 1947) suggests that associations formed earlier in life may have greater influence than later-formed associations. Families provide early contingencies for reinforcement and punishment (Patterson & Dishion, 1985), typically providing normative orientations (Bauman, Foshee, Linzer & Koch, 1990; Elliott et al., 1985; Kandel & Andrews, 1987; Patterson & Dishion, 1985). Family associations precede peer associations, except in rare circumstances, and may span a greater period (Akers, 1998). However, frequency, duration, and intensity also influence behavior, and parents are typically more influential in early adolescence than in later years (Allen, Donohue, Griffin, Ryan & Mitchell-Turner, 2003), a time when peers have more influence (Jang, 1999, 2002).

Association measures are the most common social learning variables used to test the theory, and often the only measure included in research (Akers, 1998). However, the other three concepts offer important understanding of the social learning process.

The second social learning concept, *definitions*, is also an elaboration of that presented in differential association theory (Sutherland, 1947). Definitions refer to an individual's (Akers, 1998;

Sutherland, 1947) attitudes toward deviant or conforming behavior (Akers, 1998), yet they allow that the attitudes of others may also be important (Akers, 1998). Definitions occur through contingencies of reinforcement, and they may generally or specifically favor deviancy (positive definitions), oppose deviancy (negative definitions), or justify or excuse deviancy under certain conditions despite generally opposing certain behavior (neutralizing definitions).

Once formed, definitions serve as cues (discriminative stimuli) to anticipated reinforcement or punishment for certain behavior (Akers, 1998). Social learning researchers have thus far identified, or incorporated, four definition dimensions (see Akers, 1998): beliefs (Hirschi, 1969; see Akers, 1998), attitudes (Burgess & Akers, 1966; Cressey, 1953; Sutherland, 1947), justifications/rationalizations (Cressey, 1953; Sutherland, 1947; Sykes & Matza, 1957), and orientations (Sutherland, 1947). Measurements of general law-abiding or law-violating attitudes (e.g., Akers et al., 1979), approval or disapproval of specific acts (e.g., Akers et al., 1979), and justifications or excuses for specific behavior (e.g., Akers et al., 1979; Sykes & Matza, 1957) index the definitions concept.

Imitation, the third social learning concept, stems from social cognitive theory (Bandura, 1977). Imitation represents an incorporation of modern learning theory ideas that alter Sutherland's (1947) view that imitation plays little role in criminal behavior.

Imitation involves the idea that individuals note and model the behavior of admired others. By watching others and noting the outcomes, individuals are able to deduce probable outcomes from adopting the behavior. Imitation may be more important to the onset of deviant behavior as opposed to its effect on the continuance or desistance of behavior (Akers, 1998). Measurements of admired models who engage in certain behaviors index imitation (e.g., Akers et al., 1979).

The fourth social learning concept, differential reinforcement, stems from behavioral theory (B.F. Skinner, 1953) and refers to the instrumental conditioning of behavior. Individuals anticipate the outcome of present or future behavior based on the reward or punishment of past or present behavior (Akers, 1998). Measurements of social and nonsocial expectations of the rewards or costs of a certain behavior index differential reinforcement (e.g., Akers et al., 1979).

Social learning theory identifies four concepts involved in learned behavior, but they are not equally important. Further, behavior is complex and the theory anticipates that the concepts feed back into one another through the individual thought process, affecting future behavior (Akers, 1998). Social learning theory postulates that behavior is determined by the frequency, amount, and probability of past and present environmental consequences. Akers (1998) comments,

The typical process of initiation, continuation, progression, and desistance is hypothesized to be as follows:

1. The balance of past and current associations, definitions, and imitation of deviant models, and the anticipated balance of reinforcement in particular situations, produces or inhibits the initial delinquent or deviant acts.

2. The effects of these variables continue in the repetition of acts, although imitation becomes less important than it was in the first commission of the act.

3. After initiation, the actual social and nonsocial reinforcers and punishers affect the probability that the acts will be or will not be repeated and at what level of frequency.

4. Not only the overt behavior, but also the definitions favorable or unfavorable to it, are affected by the positive and negative consequences of the initial acts. To the extent that they are more rewarded than alternative behavior, the favorable definitions will be strengthened and the unfavorable definitions will be weakened, and it becomes more likely that the deviant behavior will be repeated under similar circumstances.

5. Progression into more frequent or sustained patterns, rather than cessation or reduction, of criminal and deviant behavior is promoted to the extent that reinforcement, exposure to deviant models, and norm-violating definitions are not offset by negative formal and informal sanctions and norm-abiding definitions. (pp. 53-54)

Akers (1998) advances four separate, testable hypotheses, explaining,

The individual is more likely to commit violations when:

1. He or she differentially associates with others who commit, model, and support violations of social and legal norms.

2. The violative behavior is differentially reinforced over behavior in conformity to the norm.

3. He or she is more exposed to and observes more deviant than conforming models.

4. His or her own learned definitions are favorable toward committing the deviant acts. (p. 51)

A comprehensive examination of social learning theory indexes each of the theoretical concepts (Akers, 1998). Differential associations are so important to the statement of the theory and the resulting research, however, that some scholars (Stafford & Ekland-Olson, 1982; Strickland, 1982) question the analytic path implied by the Akers and colleagues (1979) model. Still others question the need to measure differential associations simultaneously with definitions, imitation, and differential reinforcement (Krohn, 1999).

Strickland (1982) suggested that the direct effect of differential associations is the most important predictor of delinquent behavior. Lanza-Kaduce, Akers, Krohn, and Radosevich (1982) pointed out that Akers and colleagues (1979) did not order the internal components of the social learning process. Beyond identifying theoretically derived causal linkages, they noted that the hypotheses did not order these linkages. Akers and colleagues instead suggested that there should be a high degree of intercorrelation between the social learning concepts and that sorting out the interrelationships would require longitudinal research.

Krohn (1999) added to the complexity of the social learning variable ordering debate. He noted that there is a problem with thinking of differential associations as a summary concept and including combined measures of it with its definitions, imitation, and differential reinforcement components. When viewing differential associations as a summary concept, and typically the most powerful predictor of delinquency in models measuring it, Krohn suggested that measuring its component parts is unnecessary. Krohn suggested measuring the component mechanisms absent association measures as an alternative, preferred approach. The first approach keeps differential association theory as originally advanced, whereas the alternative recognizes social learning theory's contribution.

Akers (1999) responded to this suggestion by stressing that each of the four concepts mutually comprise the major components of social learning. He remarked that social learning theory is not as concerned with how precisely the concepts interrelate than it is with explaining criminal and deviant behavior. Akers suggests that removing measures of associations from empirical tests will result in less understanding of such behavior. Akers (1999) comments,

> To say that an empirical measure can both index differential association and have the added benefit of functioning as a summary index of unmeasured processes does not mean that it can perform as a complete proxy measure for all of the other major concepts. It does not mean that there is no need to measure anything else in social learning or that its presence in empirical models renders all other measures of social learning variables redundant. (p. 488)

Akers instead suggested that a more prudent approach is to continue developing measures of the four major concepts, as well as identifying and exploring other learning mechanisms.

Recently, Akers (see Lee et al., 2004) has tested social learning as a latent construct comprising the indicators differential association, definitions, and differential reinforcement. Although he did so without much explanation, and the approach may have been utilized for convenience in order to use structural equation modeling to test social learning as a mediator of macrosocial dimensions, what may seem at first to be an apparent departure in positions may not be inconsistent with his previous arguments.

Akers (1999) posits that each of the four social learning concepts, as well as other unidentified measures, together produces social learning, and that it is inappropriate in cross-sectional research to employ structural equation modeling to parse out causality. He instead prefers to view social learning as a combined process, more important in its sum than in its component parts. This is not necessarily inconsistent with his earlier comments (see Lanza-Kaduce et al., 1982) explaining that the social learning measures have notable overlap with one another and cannot be easily parsed into a causal model as attempted by Strickland (1982).

Akers (Lanza-Kaduce et al, 1982) has previously stated that causal modeling implies a closed system that does not allow for inadequate measures and excluded variables, but he stresses that the causal approach is desirable when acceptable data exist. Moreover, Akers' (Lee et al., 2004) use of social learning as a latent construct comprised of differential associations, differential reinforcement, and definitions, rather than trying to parse out causality, instead takes the notion of a social learning mechanism whose component parts are unnecessary one step further. Akers, in using social learning as a latent construct, whatever his intent, effectively advances rather than retracts his argument that how precisely the social learning concepts interrelate is less important than how well they explain criminal and deviant behavior.

Beyond the social learning model, another important debate relevant to this book's discussion is that of rival tests and integrated theory. No single theory accounts for all the variation in crime; thus, more than one explanation is possible. Although behavior is complex and one theory may have difficulty identifying the causes underlying all deviance (A. Cohen, 1962; Glueck, 1956; Glueck & Glueck, 1950; Hirschi & Selvin, 1967; Sutherland, 1924; Tittle, 1985, 1989), multiple theories undermine the role of theory as a means of organizing ideas to advance research (Bernard, 1990, 2001; Bernard & Ritti, 1990; Bernard & Snipes, 1996; Gibbs, 1972).

Theory competition (Liska, Krohn & Messner, 1989) is a common approach to reducing multiple theoretical explanations that promotes testing competitive theories against each other to aid in falsification (Bernard & Snipes, 1996; Liska et al., 1989). The assumption is that some theories (e.g., strain, control, differential association) are fundamentally incompatible (Hirschi, 1969, 1979; Kornhauser, 1978). Incompatible theories produce contradictory hypotheses, and tests of these hypotheses using the same data result in a crucial test (Hirschi, 1989; Liska et al., 1989). Incompatible hypotheses cannot be correct simultaneously, thus the theory garnering more support must be more believable (Elliott, 1985; Liska et al., 1989).

For example, Hirschi's (1969) control theory (referred to by Akers as social bonding theory; for a thorough discussion of its empirical status see Kempf, 1993) is arguably the most important social learning theory rival. Researchers commonly pit the two theories against each other in the literature. Further, Hirschi and Akers have debated the theoretical adequacy of their oppositional theories, measurement concepts, derived propositions, empirical findings, the notion of peer associations, culture conflict, and theory competition versus theory integration.

There is much research in the literature that examines social learning and social bonding variables, among others, simultaneously on the same data. When researchers employ theory competition, social learning concepts and propositions typically find more support than those derived from other simultaneously tested theories (Akers &

Cochran, 1985; Alarid et al., 2000; Benda, 1994; Benda & Corwyn, 2002; Brownfield & Thompson, 2002; Burton et al., 1994; Dembo, Grandon, La Voie, Schmeidler & Burgos, 1986; Kandel & Davies, 1991; Krohn, Lanza-Kaduce & Akers, 1984; Matsueda & Heimer, 1987; Rebellon, 2002; White et al., 1986; Winfree & Bernat, 1998).

Some scholars argue that empirical theory competition is an unsatisfactory approach to theory reduction (Bernard, 2001; Bernard & Snipes, 1996; Elliott, 1985; Elliott, Ageton & Cantor, 1979; Elliott et al., 1985). They suggest that pitting theories against each other may not be useful because testable hypotheses are not often rival. Predictions are often vague, and accepting one theory's hypothesis does not necessarily require rejecting another theory's hypothesis (Elliott, 1985). Further, crime and delinquency causal processes may be more complex than the explanations offered by criminological theory (Elliott, 1985; Tittle, 1995). Many tests of theories find small statistical significance with questionable substantive meaning (Elliott, 1985). Thus, there are many believable theories that account for little variation in crime (Elliott, 1985; Tittle, 1995).

Theory competition has not significantly reduced the number of competing criminological explanations (Bernard, 2001; Bernard & Snipes, 1996). Theory integration is an alternative approach that promotes wide-ranging explanations by linking more than one theory together (Bernard, 2001; Bernard & Snipes, 1996; Liska et al., 1989). The goal of theory integration is to unify theory into comprehensive explanations having greater explanatory power than constituent theories (Farnworth, 1989). The assumption is that although competing theories offer different predictions, the predictions are not necessarily contradictory (Bernard & Snipes, 1996; Elliott, 1985).

Although theory integration offers an alternative to theory competition, theory elaboration (Thornberry, 1989) offers a compromise between theory competition and theory integration. In such an approach, the scholar seeks broad implications of a theory through modification and refinement (Thornberry, 1989; Tittle, 1995). The goal of theory elaboration is to extend a theory to its limit by incorporating compatible concepts and propositions as needed, increasing the preexisting theory's explanatory power (Thornberry, 1989). At its outer reaches, especially in its outcome (Thornberry, 1989), theory elaboration is similar to theory integration (Bernard, 2001; Bernard & Snipes, 1996) and may be necessary to progress to such a level (Tittle, 1995).

Several elaborated and integrated theories exist in the literature, varying by their incorporation of added concepts, propositions, and variables. For example, scholars have integrated elements from such theories as control and social learning (Akers & Lee, 1999; Krohn, 1986; Thornberry, 1987); strain, control, and social learning (Akers & Cochran, 1985; Elliott et al., 1985; Hoffmann, 2002); labeling, control, and social learning (Braithwaite, 1989); and rational choice, control, and social learning (Tittle, 1995).

When researchers apply social learning concepts and propositions to integrated theory, social learning variables typically have the strongest effect (Conger, 1976; Elliott et al., 1985; R. Johnson et al., 1987; Lanza-Kaduce & Klug, 1986; Lewis, Sims & Shannon, 1989; Marcos et al., 1986; Thornberry et al., 1994; White & LaGrange, 1987; see also Michaels & Miethe, 1989; H. Kaplan, Martin & Robbins, 1984). Further, scholars have noted overlap between social learning theory and several alternative theories, suggesting that their concepts and propositions are special cases of social learning concepts. Examples of such theories include control (Akers, 1973, 1977, 1989; Pearson & Weiner, 1985), self-control (Akers, 1998), anomie/strain (Akers, 1973, 1977, 1989; Pearson & Weiner, 1985), labeling (Akers, 1973, 1977; Pearson & Weiner, 1985), normative conflict (Akers, 1973, 1977; Pearson & Weiner, 1985), deterrence (Akers, 1977, 1985, 1990; Pearson & Weiner, 1985), rational choice (Akers, 1990), economic (Pearson & Weiner, 1985), routine activities (Pearson & Weiner, 1985), neutralization (Pearson & Weiner, 1985), and relative deprivation (Pearson & Weiner, 1985).

Most attempts to integrate social learning theory with other theories has maintained a single-level explanation: Individuals with weak social bonds, for example, are more likely to associate with delinquent peers, from whom they learn delinquent behavior (Elliott et al., 1979; Elliott et al., 1985). However, recalling that Sutherland (1939, 1947) initially intended to address both structural and processual elements of the learning of crime and criminal behavior, it seems a natural fit to attempt a cross-level integration of social learning theory, a processual explanation that expanded Sutherland's microsocial theory, with macro-sociological or structural theories.

SOCIAL STRUCTURE-SOCIAL LEARNING (SSSL)

In 1998, Akers revisited Sutherland's early line of inquiry by specifying a learning approach to deviancy and conformity that crosses levels of explanation. He offered "an integrated theory of social organization and association" (Akers, 1998, p. 325) that formalized the fragmented ideas about the relationship between the epidemiology of crime and etiology of criminal behavior that he and others had advanced over the years (e.g., Akers, 1968, 1973, 1977, 1985, 1989, 1992; Akers & La Greca, 1991; Akers et al., 1979; Burgess & Akers, 1966; Cloward, 1959; Cressey, 1960; Krohn et al., 1985; McKay, 1960). Although accepting the research approach that separates structure from behavior in order to develop theory, Akers (1998) saw value in a cross-level integrated theory that addressed the social structural situations that shape individual behavior.

Akers (1998) suggested that social learning theory mediates social structural influences on individual behavior and thus by extension crime rates. The social learning variables differential association, definitions, imitation, and differential reinforcement, with other discriminative stimuli, mediate social structure's effect on individual behavior, providing the proximate causes of crime. Akers proposed that social structure provides the environment that shapes behavior through the learning process. Referring to the social learning theory elaboration as social structure-social learning, he commented,

> Its basic assumption is that social learning is the primary process linking social structure to individual behavior. Its main proposition is that variations in the social structure, culture, and locations of individuals and groups in the social system explain variations in crime rates, principally through their influence on differences among individuals on the social learning variables—mainly, differential association, differential reinforcement, imitation, and definitions favorable and unfavorable and other discriminative stimuli for crime. The social structural variables are indicators of the primary distal macro-level and meso-level causes of crime, while the social learning variables reflect the primary proximate causes of criminal behavior by individuals that mediate the relationship between social structure and crime rates. Some structural variables are not related to crime and do not explain

the crime rate because they do not have a crime-relevant effect on the social learning variables.

Deviance-producing environments have an impact on individual conduct through the operation of learning mechanisms. The general culture and structure of society and the particular communities, groups, and other contexts of social interaction provide learning environments in which the norms define what is approved and disapproved, behavioral models are present, and the reactions of other people (for example, in applying social sanctions) and the existence of other stimuli attach different reinforcing or punishing consequences to individuals' behavior. Social structure can be conceptualized as an arrangement of sets and schedules of reinforcement contingencies and other social behavioral variables. The family, peers, schools, churches, and other groups provide the more immediate contexts that promote or discourage the criminal or conforming behavior of the individual. Differences in the societal or group rates of criminal behavior are a function of the extent to which cultural traditions, norms, social organization, and social control systems provide socialization, learning environments, reinforcement schedules, opportunities, and immediate situations conducive to conformity or deviance. (Akers, 1998, pp. 322-323)

Social structure-social learning theory specifies four structural dimensions that indirectly influence individual behavior through social learning variables (see figure 1; most figures and tables are presented at the end of their first referenced chapter). Akers (1998) calls the first social structural dimension "*social structural correlates: differential social organization*" (p. 332). This dimension captures aggregate-level characteristics that empirically influence whether a community has low or high rates of crime. The concept includes empirical correlates that researchers have used as statistical controls in previous social structural studies, as well as correlates that represent social structural indicators of a theoretical construct (Lee at al., 2004).

The differential social organization dimension further refers to social structural characteristics (Akers, 1998) that contribute to what Sutherland (1947) viewed as a societal organization for or against crime—Sutherland's notion that crime has its origin in social organization and is an expression of that organization. The dimension refers to known and unknown social structural correlates that empirically influence crime rates. Societal social organization creates environments and opportunities that differentially influence micro-level social learning variables. Examples of such aggregate social structural characteristics that influence microsocial learning environments include community size or population density (Akers, 1998); age, sex, or racial composition of a population (Akers, 1998; Akers & Sellers, 2004; Lee at al., 2004); and other regional, geographic, or economic social systems (Akers & Sellers, 2004; Lee at al., 2004).

Akers (1998) labels the second social structure social learning concept *"sociodemographic/socioeconomic correlates: differential location in the social structure"* (p. 333). This dimension refers to social differentiation. Akers (1998) notes that social groupings and descriptive characteristics of individuals, such as sociodemographic and socioeconomic correlates, differentially locate people within a larger social structure. Although recognizing age, gender, race, class, religion, marital status, occupation, and other individual-level characteristics as important descriptive characteristics, Akers views the collectivities of these properties as important social structures.

The differential location in the social structure dimension taps the aggregate of individual characteristics in order to capture social categories that correspond with differing crime rates (Akers, 1998; Lee et al., 2004). Akers (1998) models the aggregate groupings of individual attributes such as family (Akers, 1998, Sutherland, 1947), age (Akers, 1998, Cressey, 1960; Sutherland, 1947), sex (Akers, 1998, Sutherland, 1947), class (Akers, 1998, Sutherland, 1947), race (Akers, 1998, Cressey, 1960; Sutherland, 1947), poverty (Akers, 1998, Cressey, 1960), educational status (Akers, 1998, Cressey, 1960), urbanization (Akers, 1998, Cressey, 1960), and the like as direct indicators of various categories of individuals in the social structure.

The third social structural dimension is *"theoretically defined structural causes: social disorganization and conflict"* (Akers, 1998, p. 333). This concept refers to structural causes of crime that researchers have theoretically advanced in the literature. Unlike the structural correlate dimension, which oftentimes utilizes the same variables, this dimension refers specifically to conceptually defined conditions that explain the correlation between crime rates and sociodemographic or socioeconomic conditions (Akers, 1998).

The theoretically defined structural causes dimension lumps together explanations that link observed, elevated crime rates to observed, elevated abstract social conditions (Akers, 1998). The dimension taps theoretically distinct social explanations for the correlation between crime rates and social conditions such as race, class, gender, region, city, neighborhood, and population size, density, and composition. This theoretical dimension generally views social order as implying agreement with societal norms and values, and it suggests that low levels of disruptive conflict produce conformity, or rather non-conformity comes from high levels of disruptive conflict inherent in social disorder (Akers, 1998). Although Akers (1998) views anomie, social disorganization, and conflict theories as well known examples of theories belonging in this dimension, other theoretical examples include class oppression and patriarchy (Akers, 1998; Akers & Sellers, 2004).

The fourth social structural dimension, "*differential social location in primary, secondary, and reference groups*" (Akers, 1998, p. 334), refers to small groups with whom individuals associate. Examples of this dimension include family, peers, school, work, and church. Such personal networks provide the immediate environment that shapes behavior through the informal control of social environments, situations, and opportunities for criminal behavior (Akers, 1998).

The four structural dimensions combine to affect individual behavior through social learning variables. Social structure acts as the distal cause of crime, affecting an individual's exposure to norm and norm-violating contingencies, and ultimately crime rates.

Theoretical Critiques

Akers (1998) argues that structural variables affect variation in crime only in that they provide contingencies of reinforcement and punishment for individual behavior. Structure serves as a distal cause of crime, providing the individual learning environment that affects an individual's exposure to norm and norm-violating contingencies (Akers, 1968, 1998). Microsocial theories offer proximate causes of crime (Akers, 1998), aggregates of which provide group rates.

An at first, seemingly condemning theoretical criticism of the social structure-social learning model is that it treats all structural variables without distinction. Sampson (1999), for example, characterizes social structure-social learning theory as an explanation for how social structural patterns influence individual variations in the exposure to social learning variables, notably delinquent definitions. He correctly summarizes the link from social structure to social learning as involving differing exposure levels that affect the initiation, continuance, or desistance, along with the frequency and versatility, of criminal behavior.

Sampson (1999) characterizes the social structure-social learning statement, however, as a quest to list macrosocial variables that influence exposure to learning patterns conducive to crime. Sampson contends that such treatment puts social structure outside the scope of the theory—all structural variables are exogenous to the model. Sampson questions this approach, suggesting that in doing so, social structure-social learning theory inappropriately separates social mechanisms from theorizing, as the model includes any macrosocial variable that has an effect on the social learning process regardless of its origin.

Sampson (1999) objects to the "everything matters" approach, suggesting that a useful theory needs to make presumptive falsifiable statements about the social structure, as do conflict, social disorganization, and anomie/strain theories. He maintains that social structure-social learning theory is uninterested in the sources of social structural arrangements, or their theoretical ordering. He suggests that the social structure-social learning theory incorrectly divorces microsocial mechanisms from the rationale of structural or cultural sources. Sampson rejects the social structure-social learning model as unsatisfying and not useful.

Krohn (1999) also suggests that the social structure-social learning model does not adequately specify the links between the macrosocial and social learning variables. He suggests that the model does not fully integrate levels of explanation because there are no propositions linking the exogenous structural variables to the social learning process. Krohn sees potential in the model, but he believes the theory falls short.

For Krohn (1999), an acceptable social structure-social learning statement, a useful cross-level integration of macrosocial theoretical explanations for crime with social learning theory, must contain hypotheses explaining why certain social structural variables result in different levels of associations, definitions, imitation, and reinforcement. Krohn views social structure-social learning theory as currently unacceptable because it is not a propositional integration.

Akers (1999) addressed Sampson's (1999) and Krohn's (1999) criticisms by noting that the theory does distinguish structural variables: The theory predicts that structural variables associated with crime rates will also relate to social learning variables. The model excludes structural variables that do not empirically influence crime rates. Moreover, Akers points out that the theory specifically presumes that variables from social disorganization, conflict, and anomie theories will have an effect in the model. Akers (1998) admits the lack of linking propositions; however, he suggests that the theory instead *conceptually* attempts to "integrate across levels by linking the variables, causes, and explanations at the structural/macro level (that account for different absolute and relative levels of crime) to probable effects on individual behavior through social learning variables" (p. 329).

Although Akers' (1999) response is vague, perhaps unsatisfying to some, social structure-social learning is an elaboration of social learning theory and it is intentionally abstract. The theory is a cross-level end-to-end conceptual integration, not a propositional integration. The social structure-social learning model is concerned with how social learning theory mediates the influence of structural variables on crime rates, and therefore, individual behavior. Moreover, despite Akers' agreement that linking propositions are absent from the theory, and inviting others to help specify "the most underdeveloped part of the theory" (Akers, 1999, p. 491), social structure-social learning does indeed make interrelated statements among its propositions.

Sampson (1999) and Krohn (1999) may confuse Akers' (1999) vagueness in describing the theoretical linkages between social structural variables and social learning variables for inadequacy in doing so, perhaps overlooking Cressey's (1960) warning that criticism not based on research is not a valid critique of a theory, rather it is a proposal for new research. Akers (1998) specifies that variations in social structure explain variations in crime rates because of their influence on social learning variables. He explains further that this occurs because of the differential learning environments produced by societal structure and culture. That is, structure provides individual learning environments that affect an individual's exposure to norm and norm violating contingencies.

The issue may not be the absence of linking propositions; rather critics may disagree with the linking propositions as presented, or as Sampson (1999) notes, "I have a different theoretical interpretation of ultimately ambiguous data" (p. 448). Sampson (1999) and Krohn (1999) do not provide evidence that the structural variables do not operate on the social learning variables as posited by Akers (1998, 1999), rather they suggest more preferable social structural explanations for crime (see Sampson, 1999), or better uses for the theory if more fully specified (see Krohn, 1999). Sampson and Krohn do not refute social structure-social learning theory; rather they present research ideas that differ from Akers' interpretation of, perhaps even his interest in, ambiguous data and views on the role of theory.

Sampson (1999) points out that the social structure-social learning structural variables are not importance-prioritized such as in Blau and Blau's (1982) test of strain theory, nor are the propositions as a priori falsifiable as those offered by social disorganization theory. Sampson (1999) would like to see the theory better address the macro-level concern with why society has the social systems (e.g., culture, age structure, class and race systems) that it does. Krohn (1999) would like to see social structure-social learning theory better address macrosocial structure and developmental processes.

However, operationalizing the stated propositions and explicating functional relationships is the role of research (Short, 1960). Disliking the social structure-social learning theory as stated does not refute the theory; rather a compilation of studies finding no support for its propositions may do so (see Popper, 2002; Lakatos, 1978). Moreover, Krohn (1999), and to some extent Sampson (1999), use questionable examples to support their points.

Krohn (1999) uses the aging out effect (see Akers & Lee, 1999; M. Gottfredson & Hirschi, 1990; Hirschi & Gottfredson, 1983; Sampson & Laub, 1993; Steffensmeier, Allan, Harer & Streifel, 1989; Warr, 1993) as an example of why social structure-social learning theory falls short as an adequate explanation of crime and criminal behavior through its lack of macrosocial linking propositions. In doing so, though, he incorrectly asserts that social learning theory must incorporate developmental perspectives (e.g., Moffitt, 1993; Sampson & Laub, 1993; Thornberry, 1987) to structurally explain the decreasing prevalence in crime as age increases.

Researchers have not fully explored the social learning process as it relates to the aging out effect, but the micro-level social learning theory implicitly explains the aging out effect as it is, and the social structural elaboration may address the issue even more so. Although not expressly noted by Akers and Lee (1999) in their longitudinal study of adolescent substance use and their subsequent discussion of the age and crime effect as a function of age-related changes in differential reinforcement, reinforcement schedules may contribute to the aging out explanation through changing associations and the extinction of no longer reinforced behavior.

For example, reinforcement occurs when there is a balance of anticipated or actual rewards over punishments. Reinforcement has three modalities: amount, frequency, and probability (Akers, 1998). Various reinforcement schedules control the emitting of behavior (Akers, 1998; Ferster & B.F. Skinner, 1957; Holland & Skinner, 1961; B.F. Skinner, 1953, 1969, 1974). Generally, behavioral frequency corresponds with social reinforcement frequency (Hamblin, 1979; Herrnstein, 1974). Some social behavioral reinforcement occurs infrequently, however, so individuals seek behavioral choices that optimize reinforcement (Herrnstein & Loveland, 1975). Akers (1998), notes, "therefore, a given behavior must be seen in the context of all other concurrently available schedules and sources of reinforcement" (p. 70).

Much of what researchers know about reinforcement schedules comes from laboratory studies with animals such as pigeons and rats (Ferster & B.F. Skinner, 1957; Herrnstein & Loveland, 1975; Holland & B.F. Skinner, 1961; B.F. Skinner, 1953); however, there are clear implications for social behavior (B.F. Skinner, 1969; Ferster & B.F. Skinner, 1957; see Bandura, 1977). Behavior that is reinforced each time it is emitted is on a continuous schedule of reinforcement. Behavior that is not reinforced on each occurrence is on one of four intermittent schedules of reinforcement (Ferster & B.F. Skinner, 1957; B.F. Skinner, 1953, 1969). A fixed ratio schedule refers to reinforcement that occurs after a certain number of responses (e.g., every tenth response), whereas a variable ratio schedule characterizes reinforcement that occurs after a variable number of responses (e.g., after the fifth response on one occasion, after the second response on another occasion, etc...). A fixed interval schedule depicts reinforcement that occurs after a certain amount of elapsed time (e.g., every ten minutes), and a variable interval schedule refers to reinforcement that occurs after a varying amount of elapsed time (e.g., after five minutes on one occasion, after two minutes on another occasion, et cetera; Ferster & B.F. Skinner, 1957; B.F. Skinner, 1953, 1969).

Reinforced behavior is more probable to occur again in the future (Ferster & B.F. Skinner, 1957; B.F. Skinner, 1953, 1969; see Akers, 1998), and behavior that is not reinforced is extinguished (see Ferster & B.F. Skinner, 1957; B.F. Skinner, 1953, 1969). Behaviors that are on continuous schedules of reinforcement extinguish easily when not reinforced. Ratio schedules of reinforcement tend to produce higher response rates than interval schedules. Variable schedules tend to be more difficult to extinguish than fixed schedules (Ferster & B.F. Skinner, 1957; B.F. Skinner, 1953, 1969). Social behavior is generally on a variable interval schedule of reinforcement (Hamblin, 1979; Herrnstein, 1974; see Akers, 1998).

Following this line of thought, deviant behavior that was previously reinforced but is no longer reinforced due to differential associations, or other changes in the social learning variables, would be expected to extinguish at a slow rate. Extinction would occur in the absence of reinforcement, but its effect would not be immediate due to the intermittent schedule of reinforcement inherent in social phenomenon. For example, an adolescent that previously received reinforcement for theft may, in the presence of changing associations such as peer (Thornberry, 1987) or friendship (Haynie, 2002) networks, intermittently continue the response, fail to receive reinforcement, and discontinue the response over time. The amount of time to extinction would depend upon previous rates and intervals of reinforcement, producing a variable rate of extinction.

Although the example here provides a more detailed explanation of the underlying mechanism than previous researchers commenting on the observation, it does not overreach previous research. The aging out example is consistent with the findings of Lanza-Kaduce, Akers, Krohn, and Radosevich (1984), who investigated social learning theory's ability to account for the cessation of alcohol and marijuana use by adolescents. They found that differential associations played a role in substance desistance. Such rationale is further consistent with Winfree, Sellers, and Clason's (1993) conclusion that changing reference groups or associations with significant others may alter previous behavior, in their investigation adolescent drug use, through new definitions, reinforcements, and punishments.

The described process of variable-interval microsocial reinforcement schedules extends to macrosocial structure through the notion of sets and schedules of reinforcement contingencies (see Akers, 1998; Lee et al., 2004). Although the changing associations described in the adolescent theft example result in variable individual reinforcement schedules, the associations provide schedules of reinforcement contingencies. No to low incidence of criminal behavior before age 6 for example, with a gradual increase during childhood until adolescence around age 12, turning into a sharp increase that peaks at age 17 or so, and continues its decline through young adulthood until finally tapering off in mid-adulthood around age 35-36, is not beyond the explanation of social learning theory, or social structure-social learning theory by extension.

The extension of microsocial reinforcement as an explanation for the aging out effect to the macrosocial level through schedules of reinforcement contingencies may be better described by drawing on Sampson's (1999) discussion of differential associations, and his reference to Glueck and Glueck's (1950) birds of a feather characterization. In that example, Sampson attempts to reconcile the effect of delinquent peers on delinquency with Warr's (1998) account that marriage correlates with desistance in crime. Sampson concludes, based in part on a summary of Warr's position as conceding that the mechanism of transmitting behavior among delinquents remains unknown, that social learning theory cannot explain why marriage results in less time spent with delinquent peers, and thus, less individual delinquency.

When the analysis remains at the individual level, as in the earlier adolescent theft example, and Sampson's (1999) approach to the marriage example, various individual reinforcement schedules affect the emitting of individual behavior. However, peer associations, friendship groups, and marriage are meso-level groups in which individuals are differentially located. Akers (1998) incorporates this depiction in his social structure-social learning model as differential social location in primary, secondary, and reference groups, as well indirectly, through the notion of congregating with like others, part of the differential location in the social structure dimension.

Sampson (1999) asks why marriage affects individual association with delinquent peers and individual delinquency. As meso-level groups, delinquent peers and marriage may present conflicting contingencies of reinforcement. The social structure of friendship groups and family groups provides the opportunities for an individual to receive reinforcement, or punishment, for social behavior. The emitting of individual delinquent behavior depends on the amount and frequency of reinforcement contingencies supportive of delinquency, versus non-supportive contingencies.

In the marriage example, more frequent associations with a spouse who does not reward delinquency than delinquent peers who do reward delinquency, will lead to reductions in delinquency and ultimately, extinction of the delinquent behavior. Delinquency extinguishes when it is not reinforced. Upon extinction, as well as during the process, through the notion of maximizing opportunities for reinforcement, association with the rewarding spouse will replace associations with delinquent peers who reward behavior that is no longer emitted. As the delinquent behavior no longer occurs, there is no longer an opportunity for reinforcement in such an environment, and indeed conformity may result in punishment, so the behavior of associating with deviant peers may extinguish as well.

Although social learning theory is near silent on the importance and measurement of reinforcement schedules, and the social structural elaboration only briefly mentions social structural contingencies of reinforcement (see Akers, 1998, pp. 322-323), the concepts are undeniably present in the theory. Moreover, in contrast to Krohn's (1999) assertion that social structure-social learning theory does not offer suitable linking propositions to explain why the macrosocial variables might be expected to affect levels of social learning, such statements may be derived from the theory, at least as it relates to the example he used.

At the individual level, social learning accounts for the aging out effect through reinforcement schedules. At the macrosocial level, social structure accounts for differential reinforcement schedules through contingencies of reinforcement. Both refutable statements come directly from the social structure-social learning explication. Finding the question important, and developing the hypotheses, is the role of research.

Likewise, Sampson's (1999) discussion of the role of theory and his desire to explain macrosocial structure, both advances a research question rather than offering a valid theoretical critique, and additionally misidentifies an implication present in Akers' (1998) explication of social structure-social learning theory.

First, contrary to Sampson's (1999) assertion, social structure-social learning theory does make presumptive falsifiable statements about social structure. Akers (1998) notes,

The macro- and meso-level variables determine the probabilities that an individual has been, is, or will be exposed to different levels of the social learning variables. The different levels of these variables determine the probability that the individual will begin, persist, or desist from behavior, and at what frequency and degree of specialization or versatility. This behavior is translated into crime rates. (p. 335)

The statements may not be to Sampson's satisfaction, but they nonetheless exist in the theory.

Second, again contrary to Sampson's (1999) assertion, social structure-social learning theory does not treat all macrosocial variables as equal, and although not emphasized, the theory does imply, if not explicit theoretical ordering, importance-prioritized structure. In his description of differential social location in primary, secondary, and reference groups, along with a reference to sex, race, and age, Akers (1998) implies that the meso-level social structural dimensions are the mechanisms through which the other two social structural dimensions, more distal causes, directly affect individual behavior. Akers prioritizes differential social location in primary, secondary, and reference groups, along with differential location in the social structure, as more important than differential social organization and theoretically defined structural causes because of their role in providing context to the social learning process.

In sum, Akers (1998) offered a theory that organized propositions between macro-level and meso-level social arrangements and microsocial behavior. Akers viewed the social structure-social learning theory as a logical extension of previous research, and he offered a post hoc analysis of how previous macro-level research findings, macrosocial facts, are consistent with the theory. Akers did not explicitly test the theory at the time of its explication; however, neither did his critics. Moreover, the research avenues suggested by Sampson (1999) and Krohn (1999) do not go against the rationale both expressed and implied by Akers' (1998) social structure-social learning theory; rather, the research suggestions may merely fall outside of Akers' interests.

Akers (1998) intentionally offered an abstract theoretical elaboration of social learning theory. He is more interested in explaining criminal behavior (Akers, 1998, 1999) than he is in explaining societal structures. Akers' cross-level integration tries to explain how existing social structure explains crime through its effect on individual levels of social learning. There are obstacles to testing Akers' (1998) social structure-social learning model, however. Most notably, data allowing simultaneous examination of macrosocial and microsocial variables are uncommon (Lanza-Kaduce & Capece, 2003).

Empirical Validity

Although testing the social structure-social learning model is difficult, there has been promising research in this area. In one study with limited structural measures, researchers concluded that family well-being and social learning partially mediated the impact of occupational structure on adolescent violence (Bellair et al., 2003). Bellair and colleagues modeled differential social organization through the variables labor market opportunity, concentrated disadvantage, and urbanicity. They defined their structural boundaries by U.S. zip code. They assessed their model with hierarchical regression and once they added the mediating variables to the model, the effects on adolescent violence reduced, and concentrated disadvantage no longer directly affected violent attitudes.

In another study, researchers concluded that social learning partially mediated the relationship between structural variables and binge drinking (Lanza-Kaduce & Capece, 2003). The modeled social structure variables included differential social organization (urban, suburban, or rural university), differential location in social structure (gender, race), differential social location in meso-level groups (Fraternity/Sorority involvement, extracurricular involvement), and two single-index theoretical variables: integration into academics (B or better grade point average) and conflicting culture (opinion of whether alcohol is central to the groups male students, female students, faculty and staff, alumni, and athletes).

Lastly, researchers concluded that social learning partially mediated the relationship between structural variables and adolescent substance use (Lee et al., 2004). Social structural variables included differential social organization (community size), differential location in social structure (gender, social class, age), and differential location in primary groups (family structure). Lee and colleagues assessed direct and indirect effects in their models with structural equation modeling.

The three social structure-social learning studies show promise for the model, but each has limitations. Aside from their varying statistical sophistication and microsocial measures, none of the tests extensively measured the differential social organization and theoretically defined structural causes dimensions posited by Akers (1998).

Lee and colleagues (2004) tested a model with community size (rural, urban, or suburban) as the sole indicator of differential social organization, and they excluded theoretically defined structural causes entirely. The Lanza-Kaduce and Capece (2003) model likewise measured differential social organization with one indicator (a dummy-coded university variable), and their two theoretically defined structural causes measures (integration into academics and cultural climate) did not tap strong theoretically defined macro-level predictors (see Pratt & Cullen, 2005). Further, although Lanza-Kaduce and Capece concluded that there was support for the partial mediation hypothesis, they assessed their model with standardized coefficients (ordinary least squares [OLS] regression) to assess the change between full and partial models, a technique Baron & Kenny (1986) and James and Brett (1984) suggest cannot be used to differentiate mediation because OLS does not allow for causal ordering. The study that failed to find support for the social structure-social learning statement had similar methodological problems (Lanza-Kaduce et al., 2006).

Although Bellair and colleagues (2003) modeled disadvantage, urbanicity, and family disruption measures that are popular in the literature (e.g., Bergesen & Herman, 1998; Curry & Spergel, 1988; Krivo & Peterson, 1996; Morenoff & Sampson, 1997; Sampson, 1986, 1987; Sampson & Groves, 1989; Sampson & Raudenbush, 1999; Sampson et al., 1997; D.A. Smith & Jarjoura, 1988; Warner & Pierce, 1993), they indexed Akers' (1998) differential social organization and theoretically defined structural causes dimensions with only four measures. Moreover, they added an additional intervening process between social structure and social learning, family well-being, and perhaps their most interesting finding, the mediation of concentrated disadvantage, involved mediation of attitudes (definitions), not their outcome measure. Although Bellair and colleagues gave attention to the linking mechanisms between social structure and social learning, they mainly did so through the altered model that included the family well being concept.

Further distorting interpretation of their results as to the adequacy of the social structure-social learning model, Bellair and colleagues (2003) aggregated social structure at the zip code level. That is, somewhat removed from the notion of community advanced by social disorganization theory and adopted by Akers as likely to influence individual learning environments. Census zip code tabulation is a statistical entity created by the Census Bureau to represent an aggregation of the predominant zip code in a census block (U.S. Census Bureau, 2000). Whereas census blocks nest within block groups, and block groups nest within census tracts, the Census Bureau reports zip code tabulation areas as a subset of the nation. The Census Bureau does not specify its hierarchy, and they do not report its average size.

Another study relevant to Akers' (1998) social structure-social learning model is that reported by Hoffmann (2002), who tested a contextual model that assessed the effects of community disorganization and racial segregation on a logged delinquency scale. Starting from the social structural tradition, Hoffmann measured social structure at the zip code level, and he indexed community disorganization through the percent of female-headed households, the percent of unemployed or out of work, and the percent below the poverty threshold. Hoffmann created a dissimilarity index to measure segregation.

Hoffmann (2002) did not explicitly test the social structure-social learning model, though he did draw on it in his research. Hoffmann was most interested in testing community structure as the context for nested individual behavior through measures of social control, strain and differential association. He assessed his model with HLM, using conventional definitions and peer expectations to index differential association and social learning, as well as interaction terms.

Hoffmann (2002) reported that indicators of the percent of female-headed households, the percent of unemployed or out of work males, and the percent below the poverty threshold significantly affected his logged delinquency measure, and that the relationship was not mediated or moderated by his social learning measures. In combination with his reported results of testing the social control and strain measures, Hoffmann concluded that attempts to link macrosocial and microsocial theoretical explanations for crime and criminal behavior "may be slightly misdirected" (p. 779).

Like the four specific tests of the social structure-social learning model, Hoffmann's (2002) study has strengths and weaknesses in its inference to Akers' (1998) hypothesized relationships between social structure, social learning, and individual criminal behavior. Hoffmann corrected for the perceived inadequacy of OLS regression to assess cross-level effects by using HLM, a technique suited to individuals nested within a social structure. However, like Bellair and colleagues (2003), he aggregated social structure at the zip code level. Moreover, Hoffmann (2002) only used four measures of social structure, whereas social structure-social learning theory identifies four social structural dimensions, two dedicated solely to macrosocial correlates. Further, Hoffmann was only able to index one social learning concept directly: definitions.

Hoffmann (2002) acknowledged that he had no measure of peer associations, and he did not address the concept of imitation. As to differential reinforcement, Hoffmann questionably concluded that peer expectations sufficiently indexed differential reinforcement, as the survey instrument asked questions about friends' expectations about life goals. However, the measure asked no direct questions regarding delinquency, the behavior under study, instead asking the respondent to report their friends' attitudes toward conventional goals; specifically, whether they view getting good grades, graduating from high school, education beyond high school, and studying as important.

Hoffmann (2002) did not specifically set out to test social structure-social learning theory; rather he viewed social structure through a contextual lens. In sum, it is questionable that his measures of both social structure and social learning adequately tested Akers' (1998) theory. However, Hoffmann's research does question the social structure-social learning model specification with research, rather than pure reasoning such as employed by Sampson (1999) and Krohn (1999).

Hoffmann's (2002) research suggests that the social structure-social learning model may indeed be incomplete until it can more adequately explain how the social structural variables impinge on the social learning process. It seems apparent that social structure-social learning theory must address the macrosocial literature, despite Akers' (1998, 1999) implied lack of interest in the topic.

Figure 1

Social Structure-Social Learning Model

Social Structure	Social Learning	Individual Behavior	Group Rates
Differential Social Organization	Differential Associations	Criminal Behavior	Crime Rates
Differential Location in the Social Structure	Definitions		
Theoretically Defined Structural Causes	Imitation		
Differential Social Location in Primary, Secondary & Reference Groups	Differential Reinforcement		

Source. Derived from Akers (1998, p. 331)

CHAPTER 3

Crime Rate Determinants

CRIMINAL BEHAVIOR AND ENVIRONMENT

Akers (1998) suggests that social learning theory mediates the effects of social structure on crime and criminal behavior. The social structure-social learning model proposes that four social structural dimensions affect crime rates, only in as much as they affect the intervening social learning process and individual criminal and deviant behavior. Social structure provides the environment by which social learning produces individual behavior.

Two of the dimensions, differential social organization and theoretically defined structural causes, draw from the domain of macrosocial theorists as Akers (1998) specifically incorporates known and unknown crime rate correlates and theoretically derived group crime rate explanations. Akers does not, however, fully explain how the two dimensions impinge on the social learning process. Akers is instead content on noting their importance and generally describing some of the indicators currently known to correlate with crime (see Akers, 1998, 1999).

In discussing differential social organization, for example, Akers (1998) notes that this social structural dimension aims to incorporate known and unknown social structural correlates of crime, be they derived theoretically or merely identified through previous studies as having a relationship with crime, deviance, and criminal behavior. He describes the dimension in terms of "ecological, community, or geographical differences across systems" (Akers, 1998, p. 332). Akers uses urbanicity and population size as two main examples. Akers appears, in this dimension, concerned only with whether the identified social structure associates with crime, not the correlate's theoretical conceptualization.

In relating the theoretically defined structural causes dimension, Akers (1998) attends to the notion that macrosocial researchers conceptually define social structural correlates in a certain way, but he again leaves determination of the precise relevance to others (see Akers, 1998, 1999). Akers groups theoretical social structural explanations into a category of social disorganization and conflict, remarking, "both view social order, stability, and integration as conducive to conformity, and disorder and malintegration as conducive to crime and deviance" (p. 334). As with the differential social organization dimension, Akers only vaguely identifies indicators of this dimension.

Evidenced by the four reported tests of social structure-social learning theory (Bellair et al., 2003; Lanza-Kaduce & Capece, 2003; Lanza-Kaduce et al., 2006; Lee et al, 2004), researchers viewed the social structural dimensions differently, incorporating a wide range of indicators and explanations as to their relevance. More notably, none of the researchers were able to use Akers' (1998) explication of the theoretical dimensions to expressly relate how their measures influence social learning and individual behavior.

After the four tests of Akers' (1998) social structural elaboration, theoretical questions remain. What indicators measure differential social organization and theoretically defined structural causes? How do these dimensions directly influence the social learning process?

SOCIAL STRUCTURAL CRIME CORRELATES AND EXPLANATIONS

Background

There is much macrosocial literature relating societal organization to rates of crime. Research dates at least sporadically to Quetelet (1831/1984) who statistically examined official crime rate data in France. He advocated the examination of crime through the calculation of averages, rather than through examining individual characteristics. He was interested in constant causes of crime, determined through probabilities, as opposed to accidental causes, which he characterized as stemming from means and opportunities, if not free will.

Quetelet (1831/1984) reported that age was the most important cause of crime, with an aging out effect around age 25 years (peaking between 21 and 25). He further noted that sex (maleness) was a great influencer of crime (nearly threefold for males to females for all crimes in his sample), and that social class and poverty were additional leading correlates.

Quetelet (1831/1984) concluded that natural forces beyond free will contributed to crime, and that age, sex, poverty, and education, for example, were crime propensities. As Quetelet observed that the same crimes were "reproduced" year after year in the same proportions (1826-1829), he viewed crime as a "sad condition of the human species" (Quetelet, 1831/1984, p. 69). Quetelet viewed crime as a scientific law, terming his observation "physical facts" or "general facts, " and he noted that one could not understand crime until one understood the general facts upon which society existed. As such, Quetelet believed that society caused crime by affecting the social masses through its social system.

Empirical Research

Three prominent studies have tried to make sense of modern macrosocial literature, varying in their degrees of broadness. Chiricos (1987) reviewed the findings from 63 studies regarding unemployment and crime rates. Although comprehensive, the topic was narrow and the methodology was descriptive. He categorized the studies by type, cross-sectional or longitudinal, and concluded that the unemployment-crime relationship was more consistent and stronger in the cross-sectional studies. Although making few firm conclusions, Chiricos noted that unemployment affected crime differently based on the level of aggregation: unemployment had stronger effects on the crime rate at smaller units of aggregation (e.g., SMSA versus State).

Land, McCall, and Cohen (1990) summarized the results of 21 studies regarding the structural covariates of homicide. Although restricted substantively, Land and colleagues, in contrast to Chiricos (1987), examined a broad range of presumed social structural correlates. Reviewing the literature, they started with the notion that such measures as population size, population density, racial heterogeneity, and age structure were not stable predictors of homicide. In regard to all of the variables under analysis, which included the other measures percentage divorced, percentage of children under aged 18 years or younger not living with both parents, percentage of families in poverty, median family income, percent unemployed, the Gini index of inequality, and living in the South, they concluded that only one measure was statistically significant, and moving in the same direction, across all studies: the percentage of children under aged 18 not living with both parents.

Having analyzed the literature, Land and colleagues (1990) estimated a baseline model of the 11 predictors using OLS regression at the SMSA, city, and state level. Their years under analysis were 1960, 1970, and 1980, and they replicated their model on 1950 data.

Land and colleagues (1990) concluded first that the problem of invariance across time and homicide studies was due to structural covariate multicollinearity. They cautioned that future studies should attend that issue. Secondly, they concluded that the most stable predictor of homicide was a resource-deprivation/affluence index. That measure derived from principal-components analysis and it expanded Loftin and Hill's (1974) structural poverty index, as it comprised median family income, the percentage of families below the poverty line, the Gini index of inequality, percent Black, and the percentage of children aged 18 years or younger not living with both parents. Finally, they concluded that the population and percentage divorced measures were strong covariates of homicide, and that the unemployment rate and age structure were less consistent predictors.

The third prominent study that has organized the macrosocial crime rate literature is the most comprehensive review to date, as well as the most recent. Pratt and Cullen (2005) examined social structural predictors far more generally than previous efforts, and their study is the most statistically rigorous review as they utilized a meta-analytic procedure that controlled for measurement technique conditioning effects.

Pratt and Cullen (2005) examined 31 social structural crime predictors across 214 empirical studies (509 statistical models) published between 1960 and 1999. They looked both at studies that used aggregate measures to predict crime rates without specifying a theoretical rationale, as well as those utilizing a theoretical framework. The seven specified theories included in the study are social disorganization, anomie/strain, resource/economic deprivation, routine activity, deterrence/rational choice, social altruism, and subcultural. Pratt and Cullen's main findings both rank-order the efficacy of specific macrosocial predictors and identify the macrosocial theories that have been adequately tested, along with a conclusion of the theory's overall empirical support (weak, moderate, high).

Pratt and Cullen (2005) estimated an independence-adjusted mean effect size in order to control for the type of measurement used by a particular study. Rank-ordered by the adjusted effect size, the 31 crime predictors they examined (p. 399) are (1) strength of economic institutions, (2) length of unemployment, (3) firearms ownership, (4) percent nonWhite, (5) incarceration effects, (6) collective efficacy, (7) percent Black, (8) religion effect, (9) family disruption, (10) poverty, (11) unsupervised local peer groups, (12) household activity ratio, (13) social support/altruism, (14) inequality, (15) racial heterogeneity index, (16) urbanism, (17) residential mobility, (18) unemployment with age restriction, (19) age effects, (20) southern effect, (21) unemployment with no length consideration, (22) socioeconomic status, (23) arrest ratio, (24) unemployment with no age restriction, (25) sex ratio, (26) structural density, (27) police expenditures, (28) get-tough policy, (29) education effects, (30) police per capita, and (31) police size.

Pratt and Cullen (2005) found four consistently robust social structural factors: racial composition (both percent nonWhite and percent Black), economic deprivation, and family disruption. These factors were strong and stable predictors across studies that used them to index theoretical concepts such as the racial heterogeneity, poverty, and family disruption measures used to test social disorganization theory, as well as when they were viewed as a composite concentrated disadvantage (e.g., Sampson et al., 1997) measure.

Pratt and Cullen (2005) concluded that social disorganization and resource/economic deprivation theories received high empirical support, anomie/strain, social support/altruism, and routine activity theories received moderate support, and rational choice/deterrence, and subcultural theories received only modest support. They further concluded that each of the theories except anomie/strain and social support/altruism have been adequately tested, and that routine activity, rational choice/deterrence, and subcultural theory results are conditioned by their methodologies.

Pratt and Cullen's (2005) use of the term resource/economic deprivation theory refers mainly to conflict perspectives that emphasize poverty either from absolute or relative positions. Such characterization does not distinguish whether poverty and economic deprivation were pitted against one another or viewed as a construct. Pratt and Cullen do not seem to intend this theoretical grouping as a clean theoretical distinction, as they assessed poverty and inequality separately, grouped them together for the purposes of description, and warned that their study cannot distinguish the absolute and deprivation paradigms. The substantive conclusion to be drawn from this grouping is that both poverty and relative deprivation were two of the stronger macrosocial predictors of crime rates.

Pratt and Cullen (2005) use the term social disorganization theory to represent the tradition of Shaw and McKay (1942), who, drawing on Durkheim's (1897/2002) notion of rapid societal change, sought an explanation for the spatial distribution of Chicago delinquency rates in neighborhood communities. Shaw and McKay (1942; Shaw et al., 1929) at first examined Chicago juvenile delinquency rates that spanned several decades in the early 1900s. They later added more decades, accumulating Chicago delinquency data for a period of 65 years, and more cities to include Philadelphia, Boston, Cincinnati, Cleveland, and Richmond, Virginia (Shaw & McKay, 1969).

Before sharing their conclusions, Shaw and McKay (1969) stated their questions. They asked,

1) To what extent do the rates of delinquents and criminals show similar variations among the local communities in different types of American cities?

2) Does recidivism among delinquents vary from community to community in accordance with rates of delinquency?

3) To what extent do variations in rates of delinquents correspond to demonstrate differences in the economic, social, and cultural characteristics of local communities in different types of cities?

4) How are the rates of delinquents in particular areas affected over a period of time by successive changes in the nativity and nationality composition of the population?

5) To what extent are the observed differences in the rates of delinquents between children of foreign and native parentage due to a differential geographic distribution of these two groups in the city?

6) Under what economic and social conditions does crime develop as a social tradition and become embodied in a system of criminal values.

7) What do the rates of delinquents, when computed by local areas for successive periods of time, reveal with respect to the effectiveness of traditional methods of treatment and prevention, of wide variations in rates of delinquents in different types of communities? (Shaw & McKay, 1969)

Shaw and McKay (1969) qualified their conclusions by acknowledging that others may interpret their results differently. Shaw and McKay first concluded that there is a relationship between local community conditions and rates of juvenile delinquency. They noted that communities with high rates of delinquency exhibited different social and economic conditions than communities with low delinquency rates. They remarked,

[The] high degree of consistency in the association between delinquency and other characteristics of the community not only sustains the conclusion that delinquent behavior is related dynamically to the community but also appears to establish that all community characteristics, including delinquency, are products of the operation of general processes more or less common to American cities. Shaw & McKay, 1969)

Referring to the Chicago data, Shaw and McKay (1942, 1969) further noted that delinquency rates remained stable during the years under examination, regardless of the neighborhoods' racial or ethnic composition. The populations of neighborhoods with high delinquency rates were mainly comprised of immigrants. Further, they found that delinquency rates increased the further away from the central core of the city. They reasoned that delinquency *must* be related to inherent community characteristics.

Taking a different approach to rapid growth than Shaw and McKay (1942, 1969), Wirth (1938) observed that a large city represents many people that have little in common. He concluded that urbanism, the rapid growth associated with the development of cities, resulted in superficial social relations. According to Wirth, such heterogeneity may result in "personal disorganization, mental breakdown, suicide, delinquency, crime, corruption, and disorder. . . (p. 230)." Early research derived from Wirth (1938) tended to look at a city's population density, the number of people packed into a geographical area, and the various stratifications that resulted from masses of people that knew larger groups only superficially, such as race composition, sex composition, age composition, and poverty.

As gleaned from Pratt And Cullen (2005), researchers often use urbanicity or population density variables either as items of interest or as a statistical controls (Allison, 1972; Archer, Gardner, Akert & Lockwood, 1978; Bursik & Webb, 1982; Byrne, 1986; Copes, 1999; Gibbs & Erickson, 1976; Jackson, 1984; Krohn et al., 1984; Mencken & Barnett, 1999; Mladenka & Hill, 1976; Morenoff & Sampson, 1997; Osborn, Trickett & Elder, 1992; Pressman & Carol, 1971; Sampson, 1985; Sampson & Groves, 1989; M.D. Smith & Brewer, 1992; Stafford & Gibbs, 1980; Warner & Pierce, 1993; Webb, 1972). As to efficacy, Pratt and Cullen (2005) concluded that urbanicity has high strength (an effect size estimate two standard errors above the pooled mean across studies with various methodological specifications) and high stability (degree in change of effect size when accounting for model methodology) and structural density has moderate strength (an effect size estimate within two standard errors above the pooled mean) and moderate stability as a predictors of crime rates.

The literature reports frequent examinations of racial composition as a correlate of crime rates, measured either as the percent or proportion of a given population that is nonWhite or Black (Chamlin, 1989; Liska, Logan & Bellair, 1998; Neapolitan, 1998; Sampson, 1985, 1986; M.D. Smith & Bennett, 1985; D.A. Smith & Parker, 1980; Stafford & Gibbs, 1980; Williams, 1984; Williams & Flewelling, 1988), as well as numerous studies with age, sex, and poverty measures (e.g., Allison, 1972; Bailey, 1984, 1999; Baum, 1999; Blau & Blau, 1982; Britt, 1992; L. Cohen & Land, 1987; Copes, 1999; Curry & Spergel, 1988; Gartner, Baker & Pampel, 1990; Gauthier & Bankston, 1997; Glaser & Rice, 1959; Greenberg, 1985; Kapuskinski, Braithwaite & Chapman, 1998; Messner, 1982; Messner & Sampson, 1991; O'Brien, 1991; Osborn et al., 1992; Patterson, 1991; R.D. Peterson & Bailey, 1988; Phillips & Votey, 1972; Sampson, 1985, 1987; D.A. Smith & Jarjoura, 1988; Steffensmeier, Streifel & Harer, 1987; Steffensmeier, Streifel & Shihadeh, 1992; Warner & Pierce, 1993; Warner & Roundtree, 1997). Pratt and Cullen (2005) found percent Black, percent nonWhite, and poverty measures to have high strength and high stability as crime rate predictors, age structure to have moderate strength and high stability, and sex structure to have moderate strength and stability.

Some researchers have suggested, however, that Wirth's (1938) view of urbanism, particularly as it relates to the importance of population density, does not recognize that other factors may moderate the effect of population density on crime, or that the relationship may be spurious (Kasarda & Janowitz, 1974). Rather than forming an attachment to the community, or lack of attachment because of dense populations and superficial relations, individuals may instead assimilate to a community system of friendship and kinship networks over time (Park & Burgess, 1925).

Although Wirth (1938) discussed many urban factors beyond population density, such as residential mobility, he viewed density, the accumulation of large numbers in a small area, as mainly producing the other characteristics through the absence of intimate contacts and the loss of formal control. He viewed urbanicity as creating Durkheim's (1897/2002) anomie through an interplay among a population's number, its density, and heterogeneity.

Some researchers, however, suggest that an individual's length of residence (Kasarda & Janowitz, 1974), an individual's low residential stability or high residential mobility (Sampson & Groves, 1989), operates more in line with Shaw and McKay's (1942, 1969) rationale; that high residential mobility, low residential stability, in part produces the lack of cohesiveness found in a community, and that population density is not important when residential mobility is controlled (Kasarda & Janowitz, 1974).

Sampson and Groves (1989) characterized Shaw and McKay's theory as specifying that disruptions in community organization stemming from low economic status, ethnic heterogeneity, and residential mobility, influence variations in rates of delinquency. They noted that although macrosocial researchers frequently examined measures derived from Shaw and McKay's (1942, 1969) findings, such as the effects of residential mobility, racial composition, and poverty measures on crime rates, there had been no direct test of Shaw and McKay's social disorganization theory.

Arguing that the prime reason social disorganization theory had never been tested was mainly a matter of suitable data, as opposed to theoretical shortcomings, Sampson and Groves (1989) examined the theory with Great Britain community-level and aggregated self-report crime and victimization data. First, they defined social disorganization as "the inability of a community structure to realize the common values of its residents and maintain effective social controls (Kornhauser 1978, p. 120; Bursik 1984, p.12)" (Sampson & Groves, 1989, p. 777).

Next, Sampson and Groves (1989) explained that social disorganization should be measured by the effectiveness of those controls. Social disorganization results from a community's inability to formally or informally supervise its residents, so it can be indexed by the community's number and types of social networks. They measured social disorganization as sparse friendship networks, unsupervised groups of juveniles (teens), and low participation in community organizations.

Additionally, Sampson and Groves (1989) gave attention to the types of social structure that might be expected to impact delinquency. Drawing on Kornhauser (1978), Kasarda and Janowitz (1974), Krohn (1986), and Sampson (1987), they identified socioeconomic status (SES), residential mobility, racial and ethnic heterogeneity, family disruption, and urbanization as the five exogenous processes to social disorganization's effect on delinquency.

Sampson and Groves (1989) explained that SES was hypothesized by Shaw and McKay (1942, 1969) to affect delinquency through the mediation of social disorganization. Low community SES represents a dearth of the resources necessary to result in a strong organizational community base. Referencing Kornhauser (1978) and Byrne and Sampson (1986), Sampson and Groves (1989) noted that previous research that failed to find direct SES effects on crime rates inadequately measured the intervening process.

Sampson and Groves (1989) observed that residential mobility was in Shaw and McKay's (1942, 1969) original model as a disruptor of social networks that might otherwise be formed if not for the lack of kinship to the community. Temporary, transient residents do not form strong friendship bonds and ties (Sampson & Groves, 1989). There is much research on residential mobility or residential instability (Lewis & Salem, 1986; Sampson, 1988; Tittle, 1989) in the literature (e.g., Baum, 1999; Bellair, 1997; Bursik & Grasmick, 1992; Crutchfield, Garken & Grove, 1982; Fleisher, 1966; Heitgard & Bursik, 1987; Krivo & Peterson, 1996; Miethe, Hughes & McDowall, 1991; Sampson, 1986; Sampson & Raudenbush, 1999; D.A. Smith & Jarjoura, 1997; Veysey & Messner, 1999; Warner & Pierce, 1993; Warner & Roundtree, 1997; Weicher, 1970).

Sampson and Groves (1989) likewise observed that Shaw and McKay (1942, 1969) identified racial and ethnic heterogeneity as important to the model. Shaw and McKay argued that heterogeneity affected the ability of community residents to achieve consensus, and

Sampson and Groves noted that previous research that tested the direct effects of heterogeneity on crime, like SES, failed to properly account for social disorganization's intervening process.

Sampson and Groves (1989) derived their measure of family disruption from Sampson's (1987) argument that community controls are negatively impacted in communities having low levels of two-parent households. Sampson and Groves explained that two-parent households offered better networks of control both for their own children, and for other children within the community network.

Lastly, Sampson and Groves (1989) explained that urbanization was implied by Shaw and McKay's (1942, 1969) intracity theory as contributing to the capacity to establish effective community controls. Sampson and Groves incorporated the level of urbanicity into their model so that they could rule out between-community urbanization effects.

Sampson and Groves (1989) concluded that there was overall support for their model. They found that socially disorganized communities had disproportionately high rates of delinquency, and that social disorganization (sparse friendship groups, unsupervised teens, low organizational participation) partially mediated the effects of SES, residential mobility, ethnic heterogeneity, and family disruption (community structural characteristics) on their delinquency measures.

Other researchers have since tested social disorganization theory with mixed results. Veysey and Messner (1999) reexamined Sampson and Groves' (1989) data using structural equation modeling, finding only partial support for the social disorganization mediation hypothesis. Instead, they suggested that social disorganization represents more than one mechanism, and that its operation supports additional theories of crime than social disorganization theory, including peer affiliation theories.

First, Veysey and Messner (1999) argued that SEM analyses revealed that social disorganization as measured by Sampson and Groves (1989) did not comprise a single construct. The indicators instead measured separate social processes. Veysey and Messner suggested that although the construct did not measure one distinct dimension, and although it was not a mediator of each of the community-level variables, it could be that the construct works as hypothesized but was measured poorly.

Further, Veysey and Messner (1999) observed that the strongest mediation of community effects came from the community's perception of unsupervised teens. As analyses revealed it was a distinct intervening dimension, Veysey and Messner concluded that Sampson and Groves' (1989) conclusion of clear support for social disorganization theory was overstated. Veysey and Messner instead likened the peer group measure more to Akers and colleagues' (1979) social learning theory than social disorganization theory. They found the test of social disorganization theory to be important, but they suggested that future studies seek stronger theoretical measures.

Lowenkamp, Cullen & Pratt (2003) attempted to replicate Sampson and Groves' (1989) findings on BCS data 10 years newer than the data used by Sampson and Groves, thus examining the stability of the findings. Lowenkamp and colleagues used a similar dataset and measures to those used by Sampson and Groves, but they examined a different time and place. Lowenkamp and colleagues concluded that their results were generally consistent with those of Sampson and Groves, and that the general propositions of social disorganization theory were supported.

Lowenkamp and colleagues (2003) addressed Veysey and Messner's (1999) characterization of Sampson and Groves' (1989) study as supporting multiple theoretical explanations as one worthy of future research. They suggested that future research explore the mechanisms as to why the variables have the effects that they do.

D. Gottfredson, McNeil, and Gottfredson (1991) investigated the mechanisms by which characteristics of a social area affect individual delinquency. Although they used social disorganization measures, they expanded on some of Sampson and Groves' (1991) measures, and they did not aggregate the individual level survey data as did Sampson and Groves. D. Gottfredson and colleagues instead examined the effects of social structure directly on individual level delinquency.

D. Gottfredson and colleagues (1991) argued that researchers had long been interested in the mechanisms by which social structure impacts individual behavior, but that no previous study had suitably looked at the issue in light of ecological research such as that by Shaw and McKay (1942) and Sampson and Groves (1989). They further argued that two (Reiss & Rhodes, 1961; Johnstone, 1978) of the three published articles that had drawn conclusions regarding the effects of area characteristics on individual level crime used unsound methodologies: They violated Hauser's (1970) caution against a contextual fallacy, misinterpreting groups effects when shifting conclusions from an individual level of analysis.

The third study, D. Gottfredson and colleagues (1991) argued, was methodologically sound, and it offered a more complete multi-level test of the effects of social structure on individual delinquency, but its lack of broad social structural measures failed to shed more light on how the macrosocial process affected individual level behavior. Simcha-Fagan and Schwartz (1986) assessed the contextual effects of community economic level, community disorder, community organizational base, and community residential stability on self-reported and officially recorded delinquency through the intervening mechanisms of bonds to conventional social roles and bonds to deviant social groups in a sample of 12 New York City neighborhoods. They advanced their model as representing portions of social disorganization, subcultural, and labeling theories.

Simcha-Fagan and Schwartz (1986) concluded that one community level construct representing social disorganization theory and another construct representing the subcultural perspective found strong empirical support. Simcha-Fagan and Schwartz reported that both constructs impacted a community's ability to sustain organizational participation, and that the variance between group effects on their delinquency measures was much reduced by the addition of individual-level variables. They summed their findings, in part, commenting, "[The study] indicates that when the reduced-form equation is more fully specified, community effects on delinquency are to a large extent mediated by socialization processes. The consideration of direct effects of community characteristics on delinquency thus involves an oversimplification" (p. 695).

D. Gottfredson and colleagues (1991) utilized a design strategy similar to Simcha-Fagan and Schwartz (1986) but they broadened the sample of social areas by examining a convenience sample of 10 middle or high schools across 4 U.S. cities. They measured self-reported delinquency, which comprised aggression, theft, property damage, and drug involvement measures. At the individual level, they measured parental education, negative peer influence, parental attachment and supervision, school attachment and commitment, involvement, and belief in conventional rules.

D. Gottfredson and colleagues (1991) indexed their social area measures with U.S. Census block group data, conducting factor analysis on the variables female-headed households, welfare, poverty, divorced, male unemployment, female unemployment, male employment, female employment, professional or managerial employment, family income, education, farm income, and nonpublic school enrollment. They extracted variables representing two factors, labeling female-headed households, high welfare, high poverty, high divorce rate, and low male employment disorganization. They called their second factor affluence and education, which comprised incomes above the median level, high professional or managerial employment, completion of high school, employed females, and a low farm income to wages and salaries ratio.

D. Gottfredson and colleagues (1991) concluded that their study provided only slight support for the notion, following the rationale of Shaw and McKay (1942), that weak family structure reduces the control that is exerted over children, thereby resulting in increased interpersonal, aggressive delinquency. In such areas, they concluded that children bonded less with controlling institutions and reported more negative peer influences than more organized areas. They also found that SES contributed to delinquency, though they concluded that the mechanism was not community control, as there was no effect on the bonding and peer association variables, and rather than affecting interpersonal violence, SES only impacted delinquencies such as theft and vandalism.

Although measuring some concepts similar to Sampson and Groves (1989), and finding some support for some of the hypothesized relationships, D. Gottfredson and colleagues (1991) concluded that differences in social areas do not greatly influence individual delinquency. They commented,

> All [the limitations of the study] notwithstanding, the assumption that community characteristics explain much of the differences among individuals in criminal behavior no longer seems tenable. A maximum of 2% of the variance in individual delinquency is accounted for by area factors in any of the multi-level studies examined—and a more reasonable estimate is less than 1%. The results of every multilevel study relating individual delinquency to measures of area characteristics imply that most of the variability among individuals must have sources other than differences in the communities they inhabit. (D. Gottfredson et al., 1991, p. 221)

Although D. Gottfredson and colleagues (1991) and Simcha-Fagan and Schwartz (1986) were interested in the question of social disorganization, both studies, unlike Sampson and Groves (1989), examined the effects of aggregate community measures directly on individual delinquency. Both studies argued that some type of social process intervened between social structure and delinquency. The studies further distinguished themselves from Sampson and Groves (1989) as they used U.S. Census data to measure community structure. Further, D. Gottfredson and colleagues (1991) suggested that better measures of social disorganization by community might have yielded different results.

Sun, Triplett, and Gainey (2004) attempted to replicate Sampson and Groves' (1989) tests of social disorganization theory, returning the level of analysis to the aggregate level, examining the impact of community on crime rates, but using U.S. Census data and incorporating broader measures of some of the theoretical constructs. They analyzed a sample (N = 8155) that comprised 36 neighborhoods across 7 U.S. cities.

Sun and colleagues (2004) operationalized SES as a scale comprised of the percentage of the community with an income above $20,000, percent employed, and the percentage of college graduates. They measured residential mobility as the percentage of residents that had resided in the community less than five years. They used Blau's (1977) index of intergroup relations to measure racial heterogeneity, and they measured family disruption as the percentage of community residents that were divorced or separated. They held urbanicity constant, as all communities in the sample were considered urban.

Sun and colleagues (2004) measured the intervening construct local social ties as the percentage of neighbors who reported doing things together, and they measured organizational participation as the percent of residents who attended community meetings during the previous 6-12 months relating to area drug problems. Sun and colleagues measured unsupervised teens as the percent of residents who considered disruptions around schools as a problem. Their dependent variables were robbery and assault rates.

Sun and colleagues (2004) modeled paths that accounted for those reported by Veysey and Messner's (1999) replication of Sampson and Groves' (1989) study, concluding that social disorganization's mediation of community effects on crime found only partial support.

They found that each of the social disorganization measures did not mediate the community-level effects; rather only the local social ties measure did so effectively. They, like the other tests of social disorganization theory, suggested that future research employ better measures of the theorized constructs.

Applicability to Social Structure-Social Learning

Akers (1998) suggests that the social learning process mediates the effects of social structure on crime and criminal behavior. Although he proposes four social structural dimensions, two of the dimension's indicators overlap as they both seek empirically sound macrosocial correlates of crime rates, one from the angle of incorporating known correlates, be they atheoretical or theoretically derived, and the other focusing specifically on theoretical explanations. Akers appears mainly unconcerned with the source of the social structural variables, beyond their empirical relationship with crime. Akers likewise is not concerned with theoretically derived rationales, beyond noting that the most promising theories are anomie, social disorganization, and conflict.

Pratt and Cullen (2005) provided the most comprehensive and recent examination of macrosocial predictors of crime rates. Their meta-analysis suggested that social disorganization and the conflict notions of resource or economic deprivation provide adequately tested and highly supported theoretical macro-level explanations for crime. Pratt and Cullen found that racial composition, family disruption, and poverty were the most robust macrosocial crime rate predictors, and they suggested that macrosocial theoretical tests would be misspecified without their inclusion. In addition, they identified other moderate or highly strong and stable macrosocial predictors such as urbanism, structural density, age, and sex, among others.

Sampson and Groves (1989) demonstrated how to measure and test social disorganization theory, a rationale that was adapted to U.S. Census data by Sun and colleagues (2004). D. Gottfredson and colleagues (1991) and Simcha-Fagan and Schwartz (1986) showed how the effects of macrosocial variables could be tested on individual delinquency directly, though both studies modeled intervening variables that in part contained social learning (deviant peers) measures. Although not testing social disorganization theory, per se, Hoffmann (2002), discussed in the previous chapter, likewise examined the direct effects of social structure on individual delinquency including various intervening measures, some of which were intended to represent social learning variables.

Some of the macrosocial research found weak social structural effects, suggesting that future research should seek better theoretical measures (e.g., D. Gottfredson et al., 1991; Lowenkamp et al., 2003; Sun et al., 2004; Veysey and Messner, 1999). Although working from a framework different than that of social disorganization, and examining a narrow outcome measure, Land and colleagues (1990) warned that in addition to measuring structural covariates consistently, researchers must make sure that the intercorrelation between predictors does not interfere with the power of the statistical examination.

Although the macrosocial literature approaches the problem of crime from a position differently than that of Akers (1998), none of the reviewed literature convincingly refutes his viewpoint. Instead, much of the literature supports Akers' notion that social disorganization and conflict theories are important macrosocial correlates, and three studies showed how their indicators, as well as other macrosocial crime covariates might be tested on individual level data.

CHAPTER 4

Research Design and Analytic Strategy

SAMPLE

This book reports analyses of microsocial data obtained from an existing dataset, merged with macrosocial data. The individual-level data for this study come from a 1998 cross-sectional survey of Largo, Florida high school and middle school students (see Wareham, Cochran, Dembo, & Sellers, 2005).

Largo is a metropolitan area comprising 15.41 square miles in west central Florida. Its population during the 1990s was around 69,000 people: 47% male, 92% White, 9% foreign-born, 20% never married, and 16% aged younger than 18 years (U.S. Census Bureau, 1990, 2000). Roughly 6% of Largo's families had income below the poverty level, and the city's 1998 median adjusted household income was $42,000 (Largo Chamber of Commerce, 1998; U.S. Census Bureau, 1990, 2000). The 1998 City of Largo official crime rate (per 100,000) was 5,019: 3 murders, 24 forcible rapes, 65 robberies, 347 aggravated assaults, 642 burglaries, 2,159 larcenies, and 185 motor vehicle thefts (Florida Department of Law Enforcement, 1999).

The Largo public high school, one of several high schools in the area, had 1,948 enrolled students (grades 9-12) during the 1998-1999 school year, with an average class size of 31 students. There were 150 school-related reports of crime or violence that year: 18 violent acts against people; 25 incidents of fighting or harassment; 9 possession of weapon incidents; 3 incidents of property damage; 83 alcohol, tobacco, and other drug incidents; and 12 other nonviolent or disorderly incidents (Florida Department of Education, 2003).

The Largo middle school, one of two area middle schools, had 1,294 enrolled students (grades 6-8) during the 1998-1999 school year, with an average class size of 25 students. There were 61 school-related reports of crime or violence that year: 18 violent acts against people; 6 incidents of fighting or harassment; 10 possession of weapon incidents; 4 incidents of property damage; 13 alcohol, tobacco, and other drug incidents; and 10 other nonviolent or disorderly incidents (Florida Department of Education, 2003).

In December 1998, students from a random sample of 30 third-period high school classes and all middle school Social Studies classes completed a 239-item questionnaire (see Wareham et al., 2005). The study employed passive parental consent procedures that were approved by the university Institutional Review Board (IRB). All survey information was anonymous, and researchers kept the street intersection nearest to the respondent's home address (asked in order to link the respondent to a Census block group) confidential.

Although researchers advised students that participation was voluntary (Wareham et al., 2005), consistent with the tenets of informed consent (see APA, 1992; D. Smith, 2003), passive parental consent for juveniles has been controversial. In active parental consent, parents receive written notification of the study and signify permission for the inclusion of their child in writing. With passive parental consent, researchers inform parents of the intended research, and interpret a lack of objection as permission to include the child in the study (Pokorny, Jason, Schoeny, Townsend & Curie, 2001).

Researchers use informed consent procedures to ensure that individual participation is voluntary (D. Smith, 2003). Legal and ethical considerations generally require parental permission to include juveniles in research (APA, 1992; D. Smith, 2003), but participation from active parental consent is often lower than that of passive parental consent (Pokorny et al., 2001), so researchers simultaneously consider selection bias (see Anderman, Cheadle, Curry, Diehr, Shultz & Wagner, 1995).

In the Largo study, however, the researchers were especially concerned with the ethical consideration of confidentiality. The Largo police department funded the research with a Community Oriented Policing grant (see Wareham et al., 2005). As the researchers solicited sensitive information from the respondents such as involvement in illegal behavior and the intersection of streets closest to their residence, the researchers decided, and the IRB concurred, that passive parental consent best protected the identity and privacy of the respondents. The researchers did not want the police department to have access to the names, block groups, and self-reported illicit behaviors of the study respondents.

On the day of survey administration, a researcher described the purpose of the study, explained that participation was voluntary, and remained available to answer questions (Wareham et al, 2005). The survey response rate was 79% (N = 625) for the high school and 81% (N=1,049) for the middle school.

The community-level data for the present study come from the 2000 U.S. Census of population and Housing Summary File 3, aggregated at the Pinellas County block group level (U.S. Census Bureau, 2000), and from information collected in the Largo survey. The present study adopts the approach of including block-groups for which at least one respondent resided (see D. Gottfredson et al., 1991; see also, Rountree, Land & Miethe, 1994; Sampson et al., 1997).

The Census 2000 aggregates reporting areas hierarchically. A census *tract* is a geographic statistical subdivision of a county. Tracts average about 4,000 people and the Census Bureau intends tracts to be relatively homogeneous across population, economic status, and living condition characteristics. The Census Bureau defines tracts with input from local officials, and they characterize a tract as representing a neighborhood. Census 2000 was the first decennial census that covered the entire country by tract (U.S. Census Bureau, 2000).

Census *blocks* are smaller aggregates in area, such as a block bounded by city streets, and they average about 85 people (Myers, 1992). The Census 2000 identifies blocks through a four-digit numbering system, one different than that used in previous censuses (U.S. Census Bureau, 2000).

A *block group* is a cluster of census blocks whose number begins with the same first digit as other blocks within the tract. Census block groups typically contain between 600 and 3,000 people depending on the urbanicity of the measured area, with an ideal size of 1,500 people (U.S. Census Bureau, 2000).

In the Census 2000, blocks nest within block groups, which nest within census tracts, which nest within counties of the 50 states and the District of Columbia. Before the state level, the Census 2000 subdivides the United States first into four regions and then into nine divisions. Although the census collects information from blocks, the smallest geographic subdivision for which the Census Bureau publicly reports, the block group is the lowest level of aggregated data provided in summary file 3 (U.S. Census Bureau, 2000).

The U.S. Census Bureau divides reporting areas hierarchically, and it treats the detail of information similarly. The Census Bureau typically reports broader characteristics for the political and statistical subdivisions that are closer to the top of the reporting hierarchy (Myers, 1992). Summary file 3 details social, economic, and housing characteristics (e.g., marital status, 1999 income, year moved into residence) from a generally 1 in 6 sample (long-form) of roughly 19 million housing units, as well as 100 percent (short-form) characteristics (e.g., household relationship, sex, age, race).

There is no sampling error associated with the 100-percent data (U.S. Census Bureau, 2000). There is sampling error associated with the short-form data collection method, however, as the Census 2000 asks a portion of the population more questions than it does the entire population. After collecting all data, the Census Bureau weights the sample responses upward so that they estimate the responses of the census population (U.S. Census Bureau, 2000; see Myers, 1992). Sampling error varies across Census 2000 tables, but many researchers consider the error ignorable (Myers, 1992).

The present study's merged sample size ($N = 1,674$) first decreased during the coding process that linked respondents to a census block group. Students provided the street names of intersections nearest where they lived. The response rate was 83.6% ($N = 1400$). Researchers geocoded usable responses ($N = 1,188$) and assigned them a 2000 Census identification number (Wareham et al., 2005).

The sample further decreased for the present analysis during listwise deletion (the method preferred in SEM analysis; Kline, 1998; see also discussion in D. Kaplan, 2000) to account for missing questionnaire responses ($N = 1062$). The resultant sample size meets rules of thumb in the literature suggesting that SEM analyses employ samples of at least 200 cases when there are ten or more variables (Loehlin, 1992), at least 15 cases for each measured variable or indicator (Stevens, 2002), or at least 5 cases for each parameter estimator including error terms and path coefficients (Bentler & Chou, 1987).

One way researchers deal with missing cases is to impute values for missing data. The idea is that missing data may bias the sample, and estimating the value of the absent responses allows analysis to continue as if the information were complete (Brick & Kalton, 1986). Although the approach may reduce sample bias (Kalton & Kasprzyk, 1986), researchers do not recommend imputation with path modeling because the substituted means may distort variance and covariance information (see Brick & Kalton, 1986; Kalton & Kasprzyk, 1986), a key component to structural equation modeling.

In the present research, the number of missing cases ($n = 126$) exceeds the 5% rule of thumb researchers generally use to assume randomness (Kalton & Kasprzyk, 1986; Kline, 1998; Tabachnick & Fidell, 2001). If data are missing completely at random, the sample remains unbiased. The individual sample, the census-coded sample, and the sample under analysis compare, however, on demographic characteristics (see Table 1), and *t*-tests showed no statistical differences among their means ($p > .05$).

Table 1

Missing Values Analysis

	Sex (2 = Male)			Race (2 = nonWhite)			Age (in years)		
	Initial Sample	Census Coded	Final Sample	Initial Sample	Census Coded	Final Sample	Initial Sample	Census Coded	Final Sample
M	1.50	1.48	1.47	1.23	1.20	1.20	13.79	13.83	13.87
SD	.50	.50	.50	.42	.40	.40	1.99	1.98	1.97
N	1662	1182	1062	1617	1156	1062	1652	1178	1062

MEASURES

Dependent Variable

Self-reported delinquency is the dependent variable. Its measurement is consistent with that reported in the literature (see Akers et al., 1979; Elliott et al., 1979; Elliott et al., 1985; Farrington, Loeber, Stouthamer-Loeber, Van Kammen & Schmidt 1996; Huizinga & Elliott, 1986; Piquero, MacIntosh & Hickman, 2002; Regnerus, 2002), given the constraints of secondary data analysis (Riedel, 2000).

The present study's SEM analyses interpret self-reported delinquency as a latent construct with one indicator, whereas the correlation and OLS regression analyses characterize the variable as a summed index. The questionnaire asked,

"Have you ever skipped classes without an excuse?"
"Have you ever stolen things worth $50 or less?"
"Have you ever stolen something worth more than $50?"
"Have you ever hit someone with the idea of hurting them?"
"Have you ever attacked someone with a weapon?"
"Have you ever used marijuana?"

Respondents chose one of three responses: no, never; yes, but the last time was more than a year ago; and yes, in the past 12 months. Respondents that reported delinquency in the previous year further marked the number of instances. The study equates observations more frequent than once weekly (52 or more instances) to eliminate unnecessary outliers, creating a linear composite (0-312). As intuitively obvious from the distribution of frequencies in Table 2, however, normality indices suggest the possibility of skew (4.77) and kurtosis (32.84).

Statistical analyses for this research assume normality. Skew and kurtosis are absent when their indices equal zero, and a rule of thumb is there may be cause for concern when skewness is greater than 2 and kurtosis is greater than 7 (Curran, West & Finch, 1996; Muthen & Kaplan, 1992), though kurtosis is usually the most problematic for variance and covariance techniques that assume a multivariate normal distribution (Browne, 1984; Finch, West & MacKinnon, 1997; DeCarlo, 1997; Mardia, Kent & Bibby, 1979).

A nonnormal distribution may result in biased correlation coefficients that may affect interpretation of the null hypothesis (Hatcher, 1994; West, Finch & Curran, 1995). Positive skew such as that which may be present in these data produces negatively biased estimator standard errors that may result in a lack of statistical power and an erroneous acceptance of the null hypothesis (Hatcher, 1994; Jaccard & Wan, 1996; West et al., 1995).

Although the literature provides guidance in testing for multivariate normality in SEM (e.g., West et al., 1995), some researchers suggest that univariate normality is a necessary but not sufficient requirement for multivariate normality (Jaccard & Wan, 1996). Some researchers further suggest that univariate skew and . kurtosis must be less than the absolute value of 1 to assure multivariate normality (D. Kaplan, 2000). Others suggest that such a strategy is too conservative (Jaccard & Wan, 1996).

Instead, some researchers address nonnormality through the consideration of statistical tests that do not assume normality. For example, the self-reported delinquency variable represents the number of times a respondent committed a specific delinquent act in the previous year. The responses range from zero to 234. Although researchers typically treat such data as continuous, as they view such questions as indexing a continuous measure of involvement in crime or delinquency (e.g., Hoffmann, 2002), potential responses must be above zero, and in this study, they are capped at 312. Zero is the most frequent response (52%), and high counts of self-reported delinquency are somewhat rare in these data (17% > 11). Accordingly, some researchers might view statistical techniques designed for count data as appropriate.

The notion of count data refers to the number of times an event occurs. Rather than a continuous response, a count is always a non-negative discrete number (e.g., 0, 1, 2, 3, etc…). This type of response variable is common in event history analysis (DeMaris, 2004). Event count observations comprise a fixed domain (King, 1988) that can be temporal or spatial (DeMaris, 2004). For example, the delinquency responses in the present study embody the event of delinquency and the domain of one year. Researchers might reasonably consider the respondent's self reported delinquency during the previous year an event count.

OLS regression, along with SEM, relies on the assumption of a normal distribution, and count data may violate that assumption; particularly when zero responses are overrepresented and high integers are rare. Some researchers (Cameron & Trivedi, 1998; DeMaris, 2004;

Gardener, Mulvey & Shaw, 1995), including criminologists (Osgood, 2000), suggest that OLS regression models are inappropriate for count data. OLS regression assumes a normal distribution, and a large positive skew may violate that assumption.

Instead, some researchers (Cameron & Trivedi, 1998; DeMaris, 2004; Gardener et al., 1995; Osgood, 2000) advocate Poisson-based regression analyses, as the Poisson distribution does not assume normality. The Poisson distribution's variance is equal to its mean, however, and overdispersed (variance exceeding its mean) data such as those in the present study, although not violating Poisson assumptions of a skewed non-negative distribution, do violate the Poisson's equidispersion property (see DeMaris, 2004; Long, 1997). Still Poisson-based, researchers may turn to negative binomial regression or zero modified models when equidispersion is violated as they allow a variance greater than the mean (Cameron & Trivedi, 1998; DeMaris, 2004; Long, 1997; Gardener et al., 1995; Osgood, 2000).

OLS regression is not the main analytical technique in the present study, however. The present study uses path analysis and SEM to examine possible mediation effects of social learning on social structure and delinquency as hypothesized by Akers (1998). SEM is a cross-level alternative to OLS regression when both direct and indirect effects are of interest.

Poisson regression is an alternative to OLS regression when assumptions of normality are doubtful. Binomial regression, along with various zero modified models, is an alternative to Poisson regression when the conditional variance is greater than the conditional mean. Much as researchers use alternative analytic techniques with nonnormal regression distributions, researchers likewise make use of multi-level tools that relax normality assumptions.

Researchers use hierarchical generalized linear models (HGLM), for example, as an alternative to HLM for binary, multinomial, ordinal, and count data (Raudenbush, Bryk, Cheong & Congdon, 2001). However, Raudenbush and colleagues note that for most nonnormal data, a simple transformation suitably norms the distribution and that researchers typically do not have to resort to a generalized multi-level model. Land and colleagues (1990), as well as Jaccard & Wan (1996), likewise note that researchers may appropriately transform either independent or dependent variables for reasons of linearity.

Researchers have used generalized estimating equations (GEE) to model count data in SEM (Zeger & Liang, 1986), but the technique is complicated, only produces quasi-likelihood results, and it does not derive correlation structures. The approach instead focuses on mean structure, and it attempts a "working" correlation matrix (Skrondal & Rabe-Hesketh, 2004). Researchers alternatively tend to use weighted least squares (WLS), an asymptotically distribution free estimator (Browne, 1984), as alternatives to maximum likelihood (ML) or generalized least squares (GLS) estimations (see Bollen, 1989) when assumptions of normality are not met.

Much like zero modified models account for the overrepresentation of zeros predicted by negative binomial regression by modeling the predicted zeros (Long, 1997), WLS accounts for nonnormality by weighting covariance matrices. Although the technique produces unbiased parameter estimates, standard error estimates, and chi-square goodness-of-fit estimates in large samples, it is computationally demanding (West et al., 1995).

Olsson, Foss, Troye, and Howell (2000) conducted a simulation study derived from recommendations in the literature to use WLS for nonnomally distributed data, contrasting it with ML and GLS estimation methods. They modeled 11 conditions of kurtosis (ranging from −1.2 to +25.45, mild to severe), 4 models (3 containing misspecification), and 5 sample sizes. Olsson and colleagues (2000) concluded,

> The results can be summarized as follows: The performance in terms of empirical and theoretical fit of the three estimation methods is differentially affected by sample size, specification error, and kurtosis. Of these three methods, ML is considerably more insensitive than the other two variations in sample size and kurtosis. Only empirical fit is affected by specification error—as it should be. Moreover, ML tends in general not only to be more stable, but also demonstrates higher accuracy in terms of empirical and theoretical fit compared to the other estimators. (pp. 577-578)

Olsson and colleague's (2000) findings are consistent with Lei and Lomax (2005), who specifically tested the effects of SEM nonnormality through simulation and concluded, "nonnormality conditions have almost no effect on the standard errors of parameter estimates regardless of the sample size and estimation methods" (p. 16). Although other researchers have likewise concluded that the assumption of SEM normality is robust in its estimation of parameters

(Fan & Wang, 1998), Lei and Lomax (2005) further sought identification of the more robust goodness-of-fit indices. They concluded that nonnormality should not prevent researchers from interpreting parameter estimates as usual, and that the normed fit index (NFI), the non-normed-fit index (NNFI), and the comparative fit index (CFI) are more appropriate indexes than the chi-square test statistic.

West and colleagues (1995) likewise suggest that SEM is robust to SEM violations of normality, and they further argue that SEM is robust to scaling assumptions. West and colleagues observe that although SEM assumes continuous variables with a multivariate normal distribution, real data often do not satisfy the assumptions. They cite measures of the amount of substance use as an example. To address potential multivariate nonnormality, West and colleagues recommend linear data transformation.

Transformation preserves the order of observations and the broad meaning of a variable, but it alters the distance between observations (West et al., 1995), thus stabilizing its variance (Stone & Hollenbeck, 1989). Transformation is possible when a variable's scale has no inherent meaning, and the point is to reexpress variables so that their distribution looks like a normal distribution (Jaccard & Wan, 1996). Some researchers recommend transforming all variables to remedy normality, unless doing so would hinder interpretation, as transformations generally improve results (Tabachnick & Fidell, 2001).

The transformation suggested by moderate to substantial positive skew is a logarithm (log_{10}; Tabachnick & Fidell, 2001). Only positive numbers can have a logarithm, and as the present research dependent variable contained zeros, the constant .50 was added to each value before the log_{10} transformation (see Tabachnick & Fidell, 2001; West et al., 1995). Transforming the study dependent variable dramatically reduced univariate skewness (.84) and kurtosis (-.507), bringing both indexes under Curran and colleagues (1996) and Muthen and Kaplan's (1992) rule of thumb, thus allowing improved evaluation of the distribution.

The present research assessed the construct validity of the theoretically reasoned delinquency scale through principal-components analysis, using the eigenvalue-one criterion for prior communality estimates (Kaiser, 1960; see Hatcher, 1994; Mulaik, 1987; Stevens, 2002). The Kaiser criterion suggests that there is only one dimension present amongst variables when the eigenvalue (its contribution to the variance) is lower than 1.00 (Hatcher, 1994). The goal was to assess whether the six variables represented one underlying dimension (see Tinsley & Tinsley, 1987); to see if they measure what they purport to measure (Farrington et al., 1996; Huizinga, Esbensen & Weiher, 1991).

The methodological literature reports two approaches, principal-components (uses a correlation matrix diagonal) and common factor (estimates reliability through an iterative process) analysis. There is no consensus as to which approach is more appropriate under what circumstances (see Comrey, 1978; Ford, MacCallum, and Tait, 1986; Stewart, 1981; Tinsley & Tinsley, 1987), but Snook and Gorsuch (1989) conducted a simulation study and found that both methods yield similar results as the number of items increase. In an exhaustive literature review, Guadagnoli and Velicer (1988) likewise found no substantive differences in drawn conclusions between the two techniques, and Thompson and Daniel (1996) further concluded that either factor analysis approach is suitable as long as the researcher reports the utilized technique.

R.A. Peterson (2000) reported meta-analytic results, indicating that in addition to which technique to use, there is also no consensus on what constitutes a low or high factor loading or how much explained variance is acceptable. He found, however, that many researchers judge factor loadings similar to that explained by Hair, Anderson, Tatham, and Black (1998): ± .30, minimally acceptable; ± .40 and larger, important; ± .50 and larger, practically significant. R.A. Peterson indicated that in his study, the average factor loading was .32 and the average explained variance was 56.6%. R.A. Peterson concluded, in concurrence with Thompson and Daniel (1996), that regardless of which variable variance is analyzed, unities in principal-components analysis and communality in common factor analysis, neither differs on derived substantive conclusions.

In the present study, analysis of the six variables used to construct the delinquency scale suggests that there is one underlying construct (eigenvalue = 2.42). Each of the variables loaded in the practically significant range (Hair et al., 1998), higher than .50, (skip class = .61, stolen < $50 = .69, stolen > $50 = .67, hit = .60, weapon = .62, marijuana = .62), accounting for 40.44% of the variance.

Microsocial Independent Variables

The individual-level independent variables comprise measures of each of the social learning concepts except imitation, which the questionnaire did not index. Analysis of the variables used to construct the scales revealed that the skewness and kurtosis index for each variable satisfies the adopted rule of thumb for univariate normality (skewness < 2; kurtosis < 7).

The study assesses internal consistency of the scales through Cronbach's (1951) coefficient alpha (α). Coefficient alpha seeks to assess research generalizability by evaluating whether measures are reliable; whether repeated measures yield similar results (Nunnally, 1978). Cronbach's alpha is a widely used and accepted scale-construction reliability statistic, with researchers generally accepting a scale's reliability when α > .70 (Nunnally, 1978; see Hatcher, 1994). Cortina (1993) warns, however, that Cronbach's alpha can only confirm unidimensionality after unidimensionality has been established, and it should be used in conjunction with principal-components or common factor analysis.

Differential associations is measured similar to that of Akers and colleagues (1979) and Elliott and colleagues (1985). The index is a 4-item summated scale of the number of respondent friends who have skipped school, stolen something worth $50 or less, hit someone with the idea of hurting them, or used marijuana (see Table 3 following this chapter). Unidimensionality analyses for the scale suggested one underlying construct (eigenvalue = 2.46; α = .78). The variables loaded in the practically significant range (skip class = .83, steal = .80, fight = .72, marijuana = .80), accounting for 61.55% of the variance.

Definitions is an 8-item summated scale comprised of four questions asking whether the respondent agreed it is okay to skip school, steal little things, get into a fight, and use marijuana under certain conditions, and four questions asking the respondent if they would feel any guilt if they engaged in the described behaviors (see Table 4 following this chapter). The techniques of neutralization measures derive from Sykes and Matza (1957) and Akers and colleagues (1979). The guilt measures derive from Winfree and Bernat (1998). The scale measures loaded on one dimension (eigenvalue = 4.09; α = .86), with each variable in the practically significant range (skip class neutralization = .71, steal neutralization = .63, fight neutralization = .60, marijuana neutralization = .75, skip class guilt =

.78, steal guilt = .77, fight guilt = .68, marijuana guilt = .77), accounting for 51.14% of the variance.

Two scales measure differential reinforcements, both derived from Akers and colleagues (1979). *Rewards* is 4-item summated scale of the degree of fun the respondent would experience from skipping school, stealing something worth $50 or less, hitting someone with the idea of hurting them, or using marijuana (see Table 5 following this chapter). The items loaded on one dimension (eigenvalue = 2.24; α = .74), with each variable in the practically significant range (skip class = .75, steal = .79, hit = .74, marijuana = .72), accounting for 56.06% of the variance.

Costs is a 4-item summated scale of whether parents would lose respect for the respondent skipping school, stealing something worth $50 or less, hitting someone with the idea of hurting them, or using marijuana (see Table 6 following this chapter). The scale items loaded on one dimension (eigenvalue = 2.51; α = .80), with each variable in the practically significant range (skip class = .82, steal = .83, hit = .75, marijuana = .77), accounting for 62.77% of the variance.

Macrosocial Independent Variables

The community-level independent variables comprise several measured variables or latent constructs (viewed as summated or averaged scales in correlation and OLS regression analyses) corresponding with three of Akers' (1998) four social structural dimensions. The Largo questionnaire did not index the differential social location in primary, secondary, and reference groups dimension.

In describing the differential social organization and theoretically defined structural causes dimensions, Akers (1998) noted that there is some conceptual overlap based on the way different researchers view theoretical constructs. Although such is perhaps adequate conceptually, it presents the potential for multicollinearity when operationalizing and simultaneously modeling measures in each structural dimension.

Recall that Land and colleagues (1990) concluded in part that the invariance of previously reported macrosocial covariates of homicide may have been influenced by multicollinearity among the structural variables. They recommended that future research use standard definitions for structural variables and consider multicollinearity among variables.

Also, recall that the three macrosocial constructs Pratt and Cullen (2005) found most efficacious in predicting crime could be conceptualized either as indicators of social disorganization or as a composite concentrated disadvantage measure. Lastly, recall that Pratt and Cullen concluded that social disorganization and resource/economic deprivation theories (both sharing some measures) found the most empirical support, the only two theories of the seven evaluated that were found to be highly supported.

The present research operationalizes measures that indicate three of the four social structure-social learning dimensions by balancing Akers' (1998) theoretical descriptions, Sampson's (1999) and Krohn's (1999) theoretical concerns about the social structure-social learning model, Land and colleague's (1990) methodological concerns for multicollinearity among macrosocial variables, in their case covariates of homicide rates, and Pratt and Cullen's (2005) identification of important social structural covariates of crime generally, along with measurement specifications from Sampson and Groves (1989), D. Gottfredson and colleagues (1991), and Sun and colleagues (2004). Univariate analysis of each variable suggested that each satisfied the rule of thumb for normality (skewness <2; kurtosis <7), except for the race composition and ethnic heterogeneity measures, which did so after a $\log_{10}$ transformation.

Five measures index the social structural correlates/differential social organization dimension. *Population density* measures the census block-group population divided by its square miles of land area. Akers (1998) specifies this variable as indexing the dimension, and it further derives from Sampson and Raudenbush (1999), among others (e.g., Roncek & Maier, 1991; Warner and Pierce, 1993).

Race composition measures the $\log_{10}$ proportion of census block-group residents who are Black (e.g., Liska et al., 1998; Sampson, 1986). As several proportions equaled zero, the constant .00001 was added to the variable before transformation, bringing the skewness and kurtosis indexes within range of the normality rule of thumb.

Sex composition measures the proportion of census block-group residents who are male. This measure follows that of Glaser and Rice (1959).

Age composition measures the proportion of census block-group residents aged 16-24 years. This measure is likewise consistent with Glaser and Rice (1959), among others (e.g., L. Cohen & Land, 1987; Land et al., 1990).

Near poverty measures the proportion of census block-group residents aged 15 years and older with a ratio of income to poverty lower than 1.25 times the poverty threshold. The index measures relative rather than absolute poverty, in order to capture deprivation (e.g., Brady, 2003; Gordon, 1972; Hagenaars, 1991). It taps that portion of the population thought to be "underemployed."

Three measures index the differential location in social structure dimension. *Individual sex* measures the sex of the Largo survey respondents (2 = male). *Individual race* measures the race of the Largo survey respondents (2 = nonWhite). *Individual age* measures the age in years of the Largo survey respondents. Akers (1998) specifies each of these measures as indexing the dimension. Sex and age further derive from Lee and colleagues (2004) and sex and race from Lanza-Kaduce and Capece (2003).

Four measures index the theoretically derived structural causes dimension. Each of the measures operationalizes Sampson and Groves' (1989) conceptualization of the social disorganization theory exogenous variables, as adapted to U.S. census data by Sun and colleagues (2004). The present study adopts the terminology of Sun and colleagues, and like their model, Sampson and Groves' concept of urbanization is held constant, as each of the sample census block-groups are located in an urban area. Although Sun and colleagues approximated Sampson and Groves' measure of friendship ties, the Largo data did not capture such data. This is not problematic to the present study, however.

Sampson and Groves (1989) used their intervening variables to index social disorganization. Akers' (1998) social structure-social learning theory relies, as the operationalization of this dimension pertains to his theory, on the same types of exogenous variables used by Sampson and Groves. However, Akers advances a different intervening mechanism.

Moreover, had measures of friendship ties been available in the Largo data, they would have most likely represented Akers' (1998) differential social location in primary, secondary, and reference groups dimension. That dimension is not modeled in this research; however, Akers observes that the meso-level dimension indicators interplay with the microsocial learning variables closely. This research tests whether social learning variables mediate social structural variables, the effective, though not conceptual role that social ties play in the social disorganization model. The strict measurement of the theoretically derived dimension is not deemed weakened by the exclusion of the friendship ties measurement, or Sampson and Groves' (1989) other two intervening measures.

Socioeconomic status (SES) is a scale comprised of the mean z-scores of four indicators. Three measures derive from Sampson and Groves (1989): the proportion of census block-group residents with an income greater than \$20,000 (also used by Sun et al, 2004), the proportion of census block-group residents with professional jobs (also used by D. Gottfredson et al., 1991), and the proportion of census block-group residents that are college graduates (also used by Sun et al., 2004). The fourth measure, the proportion of census block-group residents that are employed, derives from Sun and colleagues (2004).

Unidimensionality analyses for the scale suggested one underlying construct (eigenvalue = 2.60; α = .81). The variables loaded in the practically significant range (income \$20,000+ = .79, employed = .67, college graduates = .93, professional job = .82), accounting for 65.01% of the variance.

Ethnic heterogeneity is a measure similar to that of Blau's (1977) index of intergroup relations. Researchers (e.g., Sampson & Groves, 1989; Sun et al., 2004) indexing racial heterogeneity use the Blau index as opposed to the percent of the population that is Black in order to examine spatial distributions that approximate segregation.

Conceptually, Blau's (1977) measure asks, what proportion of the group would have to change residence in order to have an even distribution of groups in each neighborhood. Although the measure is able to capture more than one race, recent measures have been created that attempt to examine ethnicity. Moreover, recent measures give attention to relative diversity (taking the larger group into account), as opposed to absolute diversity (merely the proportion of each group).

Ethnic heterogeneity is measured in this research through Maly's (2000) neighborhood diversity index (NDI). The spatial differentiation formula is

$$NDI = .5(\mid CW - CBGW \mid + \mid CB - CBGB \mid + \mid CH - CBGH \mid + \mid CA - CBGA \mid)$$

The logic of the formula is such that census block-group (CBG) populations for White (W), Black (B), Hispanic (H), and Asian (A) are compared to the respective city (C) populations. The White, Black, and Asian categories only include those who did not additionally identify themselves as Hispanic. The index ranges from 0-1 and the higher the score, the more segregated, less diverse the neighborhood (Maly,

2000). Similar to the race composition measure that indexes the differential social organization dimension, the ethnic heterogeneity measure represents its $\log_{10}$ transformation, satisfying the normality skewness and kurtosis rule of thumb.

Residential mobility is measured similar to that of Sun and colleagues (2004). It represents the proportion of census block-group residents who lived in a different home four years earlier.

Lastly, *family disruption* is a scale comprised of the mean z-scores of two indicators. The proportion of census block-group residents who are divorced or separated derives from Sampson and Groves (1989) and Sun and colleagues (2004). The proportion of female-headed households with children derives from D. Gottfredson and colleagues (1991), an estimation of the single parents with children measure used by Sampson and Groves. Unidimensionality analyses for the scale suggested one underlying construct (eigenvalue = 1.39; α = .52). The variables loaded in the practically significant range (divorced or separated = .83, female headed household with kids = .83), accounting for 69.34% of the variance.

Table 7 summarizes the descriptive properties of all variables under analysis. Table 8 reports the inter-correlations among the variables. Although there are many significant inter-correlations, as is to be expected with variables such as poverty, race, and SES, as well as among the social learning variables, none of the coefficients exceeds .90 (the highest being -.82), a rule of thumb for redundancy (Tabachnick & Fidel, 2001). Moreover, those with the highest correlation coefficients tend to index different social structure-social learning dimensions, an expectation explained by Akers (1998).

Table 2

Frequency Distribution and Cumulative Percentages for Self-Reported

Delinquency (N = 1121)

Delinquency Count	Frequency	Cumulative Percent
0	537	50.56
1	81	58.19
2	52	63.09
3	46	67.42
4	42	71.37
5	47	75.80
6-10	80	83.33
11-20	58	88.79
21-30	38	92.37
31-40	13	93.60
41-52	18	95.29
53-104	43	99.34
105-234	7	100.00

Table 3

Frequency Distribution and Percentages for the Questionnaire Responses that Comprise the
Differential Associations Index (Range 2-20)

Questions and Responses	*n*	%
"How Many of Your Current Friends Have:"		
1) Skipped school?		
1. None of them.	300	25.6
2. A few of them.	489	41.7
3. Half of them.	115	9.8
4. Most of them.	184	15.7
5. All of them.	86	7.3
	1174	100.0
2) Stolen something worth $50 or less?		
1. None of them.	750	64.3
2. A few of them.	307	26.3
3. Half of them.	55	4.7
4. Most of them.	34	2.9
5. All of them.	21	1.8
	1167	100.0
3) Hit someone with the idea of hurting them?		
1. None of them.	567	48.2
2. A few of them.	424	36.0
3. Half of them.	74	603
4. Most of them.	57	4.8
5. All of them.	55	4.7
	1177	100.0
4) Used marijuana?		
1. None of them.	605	51.7
2. A few of them.	274	23.4
3. Half of them.	86	7.3
4. Most of them.	109	9.3
5. All of them.	97	8.3
	1171	100.0

Table 4

Frequency Distribution and Percentages for the Questionnaire Responses that Comprise the Costs Index (Range 4-32)

Questions and Responses	n	%
1) It's okay to skip school if nothing important is going on in class.		
1. Strongly disagree	361	30.8
2. Disagree	375	32.0
3. Agree	299	25.5
4. Strongly agree	138	11.8
	1173	100.0
2) It's okay to steal little things from a store since they make so much money it wont hurt them.		
1. Strongly disagree	587	50.0
2. Disagree	338	28.8
3. Agree	176	15.0
4. Strongly agree	72	6.1
	1173	100.0
3) It's okay to get into a physical fight with someone if they insult or hit you first.		
1. Strongly disagree	262	22.5
2. Disagree	322	27.6
3. Agree	417	35.7
4. Strongly agree	166	14.2
	1167	100.0
4) It's okay to use marijuana since it's not really harmful.		
1. Strongly disagree	694	59.3
2. Disagree	250	21.4
3. Agree	138	11.8
4. Strongly agree	88	7.5
	1170	100.0
5) How guilty would you feel if you skipped school?		
1. Very guilty	421	35.7
2. Fairly guilty	253	21.4
3. A little guilty	247	20.9
4. Not very guilty at all	259	21.9
	1180	100.0
6) How guilty would you feel if you stole something worth $50 or less?		
1. Very guilty	672	57.2
2. Fairly guilty	254	21.6
3. A little guilty	165	14.0
4. Not very guilty at all	84	7.1
	1175	100.0
7) How guilty would you feel if you hit someone with the idea of hurting them?		
1. Very guilty	355	30.2
2. Fairly guilty	268	22.8
3. A little guilty	233	19.8
4. Not very guilty at all	318	27.1
	1174	100.0
8) How guilty would you feel if you used marijuana?		
1. Very guilty	580	49.5
2. Fairly guilty	162	13.8
3. A little guilty	152	13.0
4. Not very guilty at all	278	23.7
	1172	100.0

Table 5

Frequency Distribution and Percentages for the Questionnaire Responses that Comprise the Rewards Index (Range 4-32)

Questions and Responses	n	%
1) How much fun or 'kick' would you get if you got away with skipping school?		
1. None at all	436	37.1
2. A little	301	25.6
3. Some	248	21.1
4. A lot	191	16.2
	1176	100.0
2) How much fun or 'kick' would you get if you got away with stealing something worth $50 or less?		
1. None at all	655	55.7
2. A little	250	21.3
3. Some	164	14.0
4. A lot	106	9.0
	1175	100.0
3) How much fun or 'kick' would you get if you got away with hitting someone with the idea of hurting them?		
1. None at all	545	46.4
2. A little	262	22.3
3. Some	204	17.4
4. A lot	164	14.0
	1175	100.0
4) How much fun or 'kick' would you get if you got away with using marijuana?		
1. None at all	696	59.3
2. A little	161	13.7
3. Some	128	10.9
4. A lot	188	16.0
	1173	100.0

Table 6

Frequency Distribution and Percentages for the Questionnaire Responses that Comprise
the Costs Index (Range 4-32)

Questions and Responses	*n*	%
1) Would your parents lose respect for you if you skipped school?		
1. Definitely would	361	30.8
2. Probably would	375	32.0
3. Probably would not	299	25.5
4. Definitely would not	138	11.8
	1173	100.0
2) Would your parents lose respect for you if you stole something worth $50 or less?		
1. Definitely would	587	50.0
2. Probably would	338	28.8
3. Probably would not	176	15.0
4. Definitely would not	72	6.1
	1173	100.0
3) Would your parents lose respect for you if you hit someone with the idea of hurting them?		
1. Definitely would	262	22.5
2. Probably would	322	27.6
3. Probably would not	417	35.7
4. Definitely would not	166	14.2
	1167	100.0
4) Would your parents lose respect for you if you used marijuana?		
1. Definitely would	694	59.3
2. Probably would	250	21.4
3. Probably would not	138	11.8
4. Definitely would not	88	7.5
	1170	100.0

Table 7

Descriptive Statistics for Variables Under Analysis (N = 1062)

Variable	Min	Max	*M*	*SD*
Exogenous				
SSSL I: Population Density	105.80	7729.27	3811.81	1446.95
SSSL I: Race Composition (Black)*	-5.00	-.02	-2.07	1.34
SSSL I: Sex Composition (Male)	0.36	0.54	0.47	0.03
SSSL I: Age Composition (16-24)	0.00	0.24	0.08	0.03
SSSL I: Near Poverty	0.01	0.65	0.14	0.08
SSSL II: Individual Sex (Male)	1.00	2.00	1.47	0.50
SSSL II: Individual Race (nonWhite)	1.00	2.00	1.20	0.40
SSSL II: Individual Age	11.00	19.00	13.87	1.97
SSSL III: SES**	-4.38	1.76	0.00	0.79
SSSL III: Ethnic Heterogeneity*	-2.10	-.03	-1.30	0.42
SSSL III: Residential Mobility	0.21	0.79	0.49	0.10
SSSL III: Family Disruption**	-2.05	3.57	0.00	0.82
Intervening				
Differential Associations	4.00	20.00	7.73	3.51
Definitions	8.00	32.00	16.54	5.86
Rewards	4.00	16.00	7.76	3.25
Costs	4.00	16.00	8.04	3.06
Dependent				
Delinquency*	-.30	2.37	0.28	0.70

Note. *$\log_{10}$ transformation   **scores based on mean *z*-scores

Table 8

Inter-correlations Among Explanatory Variables (N = 1062)

Variable	1	2	3	4	5	6	7	8	9	10	11	12	13	14	15	16
1. SSSL I: Population Density	—	.34*	.00	.25*	.28*	-.02	.01	-.07*	-.40*	-.08*	.13*	.09*	.01	.00	.04	.04
2. SSSL I: Log_{10} Race Composition		—	.24*	.47*	.51*	.01	.18*	-.08*	-.58*	.36*	.16*	.49*	-.02	-.02	.03	.08*
3. SSSL I: Sex Composition			—	.32*	.14*	-.02	.07*	-.03	-.02	.20*	.19*	.25*	-.03	-.01	-.01	-.02
4. SSSL I: Age Composition				—	.43*	-.05	.20*	-.03	-.36*	.52*	.08*	.33*	-.03	-.05	-.04	.04
5. SSSL I: Near Poverty					—	.00	.18*	-.11*	-.82*	.61*	.36*	.75*	-.04	-.01	.04	.05*
6. SSSL II: Individual Sex						—	-.08*	.04	-.02	-.01	-.02	.01	.12*	.22*	.14*	.08*
7. SSSL II: Individual Race							—	-.03	-.22*	.30*	-.01	.17*	.01	.00	.06*	.07*
8. SSSL II: Individual Age								—	.07*	-.07*	-.05*	-.08*	.24*	.24*	.01	.01
9. SSSL III: SES									—	-.46*	-.37*	-.71*	-.00	-.03	-.08*	-.08*
10. SSSL III: Log_{10} Ethnic Heterogeneity										—	.05*	.45*	-.06*	-.03	.01	.03
11. SSSL III: Resdiential Mobility											—	.41*	-.02	-.02	.01	.03
12. SSSL III: Family Disruption												—	-.02	.01	.04	.06*
13. Differential Associations													—	.67*	.51*	.24*
14. Definitions														—	.65*	.37*
15. Rewards															—	.25*
16. Costs																—

Note: * p < .05 (one-tailed t-test)

CHAPTER 5

The Case for Moderating Effects

PRELIMINARY EVIDENCE ON RELATIONSHIPS

Bivariate Correlations

Table 9 reports the zero-order correlations between the social structure-social learning variables and $\log_{10}$ delinquency (the explanatory variable inter-correlations were depicted in Table 8). Ten of the 16 variables predicted to affect delinquency are statistically significant bivariate correlates.

As noted earlier in a different context, one way to view the strength of a statistically significant zero-order correlate is through a continuum described by Franzblau (1958) and Hinkle and colleagues (1988). A coefficient absolute value between zero and .20 suggests *no* or *negligible* correlation, .20 to .40 suggests *low* correlation, .40 to .60 suggests *moderate* correlation, .60 to .80 suggests *marked* correlation, and .80 to 1.00 suggests *high* correlation.

Three of the five social structure-social learning differential social organization dimension variables are bivariate correlates of $\log_{10}$ delinquency: population density, $\log_{10}$ race composition, and age composition. However, each correlation is negligible; moreover, all three correlations are in the direction opposite of that hypothesized. Each of the three differential location in the social structure variables are bivariate correlates of the delinquency measure, though individual sex and individual race are so negligibly, and race is in the direction opposite of that hypothesized. Individual age correlates weakly in the direction expected. All of the theoretically defined structural causes variables are statistically non-significant as bivariate correlates of $\log_{10}$ delinquency.

At the microsocial level, differential associations, rewards, and costs each correlate in the direction hypothesized with $\log_{10}$ delinquency moderately. Definitions do so markedly.

OLS Regression Models

Following the procedures of Friedrich (1982), consistent with Baron and Kenny (1986), Braumoeller (2004), Clearly and Kessler (1982), J. Cohen and Cohen (1983), James and Brett (1984), and Judd and colleagues (2001), the present research examines moderation through OLS regression. The analyses incorporate a multiplicative term in a regression model that contains both a social structure-social learning dimension predictor and a suspected social learning moderator.

The SES and family disruption models do not report standardized coefficients because those scales are comprised of z-scores. Such measurements are already standardized, and Friedrich (1982) recommends not reporting the standardized coefficients produced by OLS regression because the interpretation is not the same as that normally implied. Tables 10-21 report the results of the moderator regression models for each social structural dimension indicator and each social learning measure.

Despite the inclusion of coefficients and R-squared in each model, these analyses only test for moderation. If the interaction path is significant, a moderator relationship is supported, regardless of the significance, or not, of the other two paths (Baron & Kenny, 1986). Moreover, the paths between individual social structure and social learning variables are not interpreted the same way that they would be in a traditional OLS model meant to assess random effects (see Baron & Kenny, 1986; Braumoeller, 2004).

In the OLS moderation models, the general equation is

$$Y = \beta_0 + \beta_1 X_1 + \beta_2 X_2 + \beta_3 X_1 X_2 + \varepsilon$$

In this type of model, B_3 represents the impact of a joint increase in X_1 and X_2 on Y. β_1 and β_2 are lower order terms in the model, and their coefficients do not represent the impacts of X_1 on Y or X_2 on Y generally. Instead, the coefficients represent the impact of X_1 on Y when $X_2 = 0$ or X_2 on Y when $X_1 = 0$ (see Braumoeller, 2004). Consequently, it is incorrect to think of $\beta_1 X_1$ and $\beta_2 X_2$ as the main effects of the model, compared to $\beta_3 X_1 X_2$ as the interaction effects of the model (Friedrich, 1982). Instead, the X_1 and X_2 equations in the model are useless to the moderation hypothesis (see Baron & Kenny, 1986; Braumoeller, 2004; Friedrich, 1982).

Each social structure-social learning dimension has at least one indicator with a statistically significant multiplicative term. In the differential social organization dimension, population density statistically interacts with differential associations and with definitions to jointly reduce $\log_{10}$ delinquency; race composition statistically interacts with costs to jointly reduce $\log_{10}$ delinquency; and age composition statistically interacts with differential associations to jointly reduce $\log_{10}$ delinquency.

One differential location in social structure indicator, individual sex, statistically interacts separately with differential associations, definitions, and costs to jointly increase the delinquency measure. The theoretically defined SES structural causes measure statistically interacts with the social learning measure of definitions to jointly increase $\log_{10}$ delinquency, whereas the statistical interaction between ethnic heterogeneity and definitions jointly decrease the delinquency measure.

DIRECT AND INDIRECT EFFECTS

Initial and Revised Measurement Models

The implications of the moderation analyses are not straightforward. Although the OLS regression models lend support to several of the moderator hypotheses, albeit some in directions differently than that expected, some variables in each dimension have statistically non-significant multiplicative terms, indicating that tests of the mediational model are warranted.

Following the procedures of James and Brett (1984), consistent with Baron and Kenny (1986), MacKinnon and colleagues (2002), and Shrout and Bolger (2002), the present research examines mediation through path analytic techniques. The study follows Anderson and Gerbing's (1988) two-step approach of trying to establish a measurement model before examining a structural model.

Structural equation modeling is sensitive to one-indicator models, and further, a fully saturated model has an infinite number of possible solutions that do not allow fit assessment. One way to address the issue of numerous one-indicator measures is to assess a path model of manifest variables. Figure 23 depicts an example using population density as the exogenous variable and differential associations as the intervening variable.

Two problems occur from this approach. First, the model is fully saturated, thus not allowing for an assessment of fit. Second, the model assumes no measurement error, thereby not distinguishing itself meaningfully from OLS regression.

Lee and colleagues (2004) presumably addressed these issues in their test of Akers' (1998) social structure-social learning model through their parsimonious inclusion of a latent social learning construct. The logic of such a measure is that as social learning variables tend to correlate with one another (see discussions in Akers, 1998, 1999), they represent a higher social learning factor. By incorporating the construct social learning in their SEM model and testing the mediation of factors, Lee and colleagues avoided having an intervening one-indicator variable, a situation problematic to SEM analysis (see Hatcher, 1994), and they were able to attend the issue of saturation by constraining an index path in each latent variable.

The present research follows Lee and colleagues' (2004) example by constructing a latent social learning variable. Its construct validity is assessed by factor analysis. Principal-components analysis and factor analysis are similar techniques that tend to produce similar results, though differing in their conceptualization of the underlying causal structure (see Hatcher, 1994).

Principal-components analysis was used earlier to assess the survey and social structural scales because the measures were viewed as additively creating a higher factor. In contrast, the social learning construct implies an underlying causal structure that exerts influence on the observed variables. Despite the different conceptualization, recall that researchers evaluate both approaches similarly.

In the present research, analyses suggest that differential associations, definitions, rewards, and costs underlie one construct (eigenvalue = 1.85). The factor loadings for differential associations (.72), definitions (.84) and rewards (.70) each satisfy Hair and colleague's (1998) criteria as being practically significant, whereas the costs loading (.37) falls in their minimally acceptable range.

Researchers using SEM typically ignore factor loadings lower than .40 (Hatcher, 1994); however, recall that the costs measure was statistically significant in several of the OLS regression models (Tables

10, 13, 16, 17, 18, 21), including as a moderator to variables in the differential social organization (Tables, 11, 14) and differential location in the social structure (Table 15) dimensions. Dropping the costs measure risks altering the theoretical meaning of the construct, as well as the substantive findings of the research.

Figure 24 depicts the hypothesized social structure-social learning measurement model. A metric is established for each factor by fixing its variance at one, and each construct is allowed to covary. Table 22 presents the a priori goodness of fit measures, including the chi-square test statistic as a frame of reference.

The goodness of fit analysis implies that the initial measurement model is a poor fit (RMSEA > .06; NFI, NNFI < .90; CFI < .95). The indexes suggest that the model is little different from a null model.

Although identifying the measurement model is a confirmatory technique, one tool researchers have available in SEM is the ability to revise the model (Hatcher, 1994). Although that option is limited in this research as the model derives from Akers' (1998) theoretical assertions, examining each dimension individually may aid in the measurement model identification.

Figure 25 depicts a stand-alone measurement model for differential social organization. Table 23 reports its goodness of fit indexes. Individually, the model for this dimension still fits the data poorly. All measures fall outside of Bentler (1989) and Hu and Bentler's (1998) cutoff points for suggesting a good model fit.

An examination of the factor loadings revealed that sex composition is the only variable that is not statistically significant. Akers (1998) asserts that this dimension represents social structural variables that empirically influence delinquency, and that social learning variables will mediate their effects. In addition to not being significant in the measurement model, recall that sex composition was not significant in any of the OLS moderator models (Table 12).

Table 24 reports the goodness of fit indexes for a revised differential social organization measurement model in which the sex composition variable path is fixed at zero (removed from the equation). Each of the index values in the revised model meet Bentler (1989) and Hu and Bentler's (1998) adopted a priori cutoffs for suggesting a good model fit.

Figure 26 visually depicts the differential location in the social structure measurement model, and Table 25 provides the values for its goodness of fit tests. The model results for this dimension are mixed. Although the index value satisfies the Bentler (1989) and Hu and Bentler (1998) criterion for the NFI, the values for the RMSEA, as well as the two measures that take the large sample size into account, the NNFI and CFI, suggest a poor model fit.

Lastly, Figure 27 shows the theoretically defined structural causes individual measurement model, and Table 26 reports the results from the goodness of fit tests. The findings are mixed. Three of the four indexes suggest a good fitting model according to the a priori criteria, but the RMSEA value falls outside of Hu and Bentler's (1998) specified range.

Analyses of each dimension individually suggest that the overall measurement model needs revision to account for the differential social organization null path to sex composition. Further, although neither the differential location in the social structure or the theoretically defined structural causes dimensions satisfied all four a priori criteria for indicating a good fitting model, each dimension had at least one indicator that suggested a good fit.

Figure 28 presents a revised social structure-social learning measurement model with the sex composition path removed from the model. Table 27 presents the goodness of fit indexes.

The indexes suggest that the revised model does not fit the data. Although the measurement models representing differential location in the social structure and theoretically defined structural causes did not satisfy the four criteria set a priori as suggesting a good model fit, the indexes did suggest that the models require further examination. Table 28 describes the properties of the three measurement models.

Structural Models

The analyses now turn toward testing its structural model. In SEM, standardized loadings represent the standardized correlation coefficient for a latent construct's manifest variable indicator (Hatcher, 1994). The one-indicator variables suggest no measurement error because the measurement models did not estimate their variances. Those paths were set at one. The indicator reliability represents the square of the standardized loading (Hatcher, 1994). The composite reliability equates to the rationale of Cronbach's (1951) alpha, reflecting internal consistency. Similarly, researchers seek a composite reliability coefficient greater than .70 (Hatcher, 1994). The index labeled "variance extracted" estimates the amount of variance that is not due to measurement error. Fornell and Larcker recommend that the value for a suitable model be greater than .50.

Figures 29-31 depict the three tested structural models, and Table 29 presents their goodness of fit indexes. The criteria for selecting which variable to set the path equal to one derive from Joreskog & Sorbom (1989), who suggest picking the variable that best represents the factor.

In this research, the paths set equal to one are the indicator paths for the variables with the highest measurement model factor loading. Although sex composition was dropped from an earlier model because it contributed nothing to the construct it was meant to measure, the circumstances for the non-significant differential social organization population density loading are different. Beyond its non-significant factor loading, the race composition indicator was further non-significant in all OLS moderator models. The population density variable, in contrast, was statistically significant as part of an interaction term with both differential associations and definitions (see Table 10). This research reasons that removing this variable from analysis risks altering if not the theoretical meaning of the construct, the substantive empirical findings.

In sum, the first overall social structure-social learning measurement model appeared to fit the data poorly. Each dimension was examined individually, and a revised measurement model was tested with the sex composition path affixed at zero. The revised model still fit the data poorly, but the individual dimension analyses suggested that the revised differential social organization measurement model was a good fit with the data. Further, the other two dimensions, although not satisfying the a priori criteria for a good model fit, had at least one indicator suggest a good fit.

Structural models were estimated for each social structure-social learning dimension individually. None of the three dimensions satisfied the a priori criteria for a good model fit. Although the differential location in the social structure's NFI suggested that the model reasonably fit the data, the NNFI, the criterion that corrects for large sample sizes, suggests that the model fits the data poorly.

Table 9

Zero-Order Correlations for the Explanatory Variables and Log $_{10}$ Delinquency (N = 1062)

Variable	Coefficient
1. SSSL I: Population Density	-.06*
2. SSSL I: Log$_{10}$ Race Composition	-.07*
3. SSSL I: Sex Composition	-.05
4. SSSL I: Age Composition	-.06*
5. SSSL I: Near Poverty	-.04
6. SSSL II: Individual Sex	.14*
7. SSSL II: Individual Race	-.06*
8. SSSL II: Individual Age	.27*
9. SSSL III: SES	.03
10. SSSL III: Log$_{10}$ Ethnic Heterogeneity	-.05
11. SSSL III: Resdiential Mobility	.01
12. SSSL III: Family Disruption	-.04
13. Differential Associations	.58*
14. Definitions	.61*
15. Rewards	.38*
16. Costs	.22*

Note: * $p < .05$ (one-tailed t-test)

Table 10

OLS Regression Dimension I (Population Density) Moderator Models (N = 1062)

		Model		
Independent Variables		b	$se(b)$	B
Population Density		4.32E-05	.00	.09
Differential Association		.15	.01	.77*
(Population Density) X (Differential Association)		-1.00E-05	.00	**-.26***
Intercept		-.77*	.12	
R^2	.35			
$F\ (p < .05)$	186.65			
Population Density		5.35E-05	.00	.11
Definitions		.09	.01	.78*
(Population Density) X (Definitions)		-5.23E-06	.00	**-.25***
Intercept		-1.12*	.14	
R^2	.39			
$F\ (p < .05)$	220.72			
Population Density		-1.16E-05	.00	-.02
Rewards		.10	.02	.78*
(Population Density) X (Rewards)		-3.62E-06	.00	-.09
Intercept		-.32*	.14	
R^2	.15			
$F\ (p < .05)$	64.13			
Population Density		1.38E-05	.00	.03
Costs		.08	.02	.33*
(Population Density) X (Costs)		-6.13E-06	.00	-.15
Intercept		-.32	.16	
R^2	.06			
$F\ (p < .05)$	21.07			

*$p < .05$ (one-tailed tests); significant interactions in bold

Table 11

OLS Regression Dimension I (Log $_{10}$ Race Composition) Moderator Models (N = 1062)

Independent Variables		Model		
		b	$se(b)$	B
Log$_{10}$ Race Composition		.02	.03	.04
Differential Association		.10	.01	.52*
(Log$_{10}$ Race Composition) X (Differential Association)		-.01	.00	-.12
Intercept		-.57*	.08	
R^2	.34			
F ($p < .05$)	182.02			
Log$_{10}$ Race Composition		.03	.04	.05
Definitions		.07	.01	.55*
(Log$_{10}$ Race Composition) X (Definitions)		-.00	.00	-.13
Intercept		-.87*	.09	
R^2	.38			
F ($p < .05$)	217.13			
Log$_{10}$ Race Composition		-.06	.04	-.12
Rewards		.09	.01	.42*
(Log$_{10}$ Race Composition) X (Rewards)		.00	.01	.06
Intercept		-.49*	.09	
R^2	.15			
F ($p < .05$)	63.68			
Log$_{10}$ Race Composition		.04	.04	.08
Costs		.03	.01	.13*
(Log$_{10}$ Race Composition) X (Costs)		-.01	.01	**-.20***
Intercept		-.05	.11	
R^2	.06			
F ($p < .05$)	22.79			

*$p < .05$ (one-tailed tests); significant interactions in bold

Table 12

OLS Regression Dimension I (Sex Composition) Moderator Models (N = 1062)

Independent Variables		b	$se(b)$	B
Sex Composition		-.31	1.46	-.01
Differential Association		.15	.08	.73
(Sex Composition) X (Differential Association)		-.06	.17	-.15
Intercept		-.46	.69	
R^2	.34			
F ($p < .05$)	179.51			
Sex Composition		-.70	1.72	-.03
Definitions		.08	.05	.68
(Sex Composition) X (Definitions)		-.02	.10	-.07
Intercept		-.59	.82	
R^2	.38			
F ($p < .05$)	214.60			
Sex Composition		-2.56	1.72	-.11
Rewards		-.01	.10	-.05
(Sex Composition) X (Rewards)		.19	.21	.44
Intercept		.86	.82	
R^2	.15			
F ($p < .05$)	62.02			
Sex Composition		.28	2.00	.01
Costs		.13	.11	.56
(Sex Composition) X (Costs)		-.17	.24	-.35
Intercept		-.26	.95	
R^2	.05			
F ($p < .05$)	19.27			

*$p < .05$ (one-tailed tests); significant interactions in bold

Table 13

OLS Regression Dimension I (Age Composition) Moderator Models (N = 1062)

| | | Model | |
Independent Variables	b	$se(b)$	B
Age Composition	2.28	1.24	.10
Differential Association	.15	.01	.75*
(Age Composition) X (Differential Association)	-.44	.14	**-.25***
Intercept	-.79*	.11	
R^2	.35		
$F\ (p < .05)$	185.84		
Age Composition	2.27	1.60	.10
Definitions	.09	.01	.73*
(Age Composition) X (Definitions)	-.18	.09	-.18
Intercept	-.1.10*	.13	
R^2	.38		
$F\ (p < .05)$	215.65		
Age Composition	-1.93	1.65	-.09
Rewards	.07	.02	.33*
(Age Composition) X (Rewards)	.14	.20	.07
Intercept	-.21	.14	
R^2	.15		
$F\ (p < .05)$	61.69		
Age Composition	.75	1.89	.03
Costs	.07	.02	.32*
(Age Composition) X (Costs)	-.27	.22	-.14
Intercept	-.19	.16	
R^2	.06		
$F\ (p < .05)$	20.49		

$*p < .05$ (one-tailed tests); significant interactions in bold

Table 14

OLS Regression Dimension I (Near Poverty) Moderator Models (N = 1062)

Independent Variables		Model		
		b	$se(b)$	B
Near Poverty		.60	.51	.07
Differential Association		.13	.01	.65*
(Near Poverty) X (Differential Association)		-.10	.06	-.12
Intercept		-.69*	.08	
R^2	.34			
$F\ (p < .05)$	180.27			
Near Poverty		.50	.63	.06
Definitions		.08	.01	.68*
(Near Poverty) X (Definitions)		-.05	.04	-.11
Intercept		-.99*	.10	
R^2	.38			
$F\ (p < .05)$	215.15			
Near Poverty		-.55	.62	-.07
Rewards		.08	.01	.38*
(Near Poverty) X (Rewards)		.01	.07	.01
Intercept		-.28*	.10	
R^2	.15			
$F\ (p < .05)$	62.41			
Near Poverty		.21	.72	.03
Costs		.06	.01	.28*
(Near Poverty) X (Costs)		-.08	.08	-.10
Intercept		-.16	.12	
R^2	.05			
$F\ (p < .05)$	19.87			

*p < .05 (one-tailed tests); significant interactions in bold

Table 15

OLS Regression Dimension II (Individual Sex) Moderator Models (N = 1062)

Independent Variables	Model		
	b	$se(b)$	B
Individual Sex	-.11	.09	-.08
Differential Association	.07	.02	.37*
(Individual Sex) X (Differential Association)	.03	.01	.27*
Intercept	-.43*	.14	
R^2	.35		
$F (p < .05)$	185.39		
Individual Sex	-.26	.10	-.19*
Definitions	.05	.01	.42*
(Individual Sex) X (Definitions)	.02	.01	.31*
Intercept	-.54*	.16	
R^2	.38		
$F (p < .05)$	216.76		
Individual Sex	.01	.10	.00
Rewards	.06	.02	.27*
(Individual Sex) X (Rewards)	.01	.01	.14
Intercept	-.34*	.16	
R^2	.16		
$F (p < .05)$	64.62		
Individual Sex	-.05	.12	-.04
Costs	.01	.02	.04
(Individual Sex) X (Costs)	.03	.01	.25*
Intercept	-.04	.18	
R^2	.07		
$F (p < .05)$	25.10		

*$p < .05$ (one-tailed tests); significant interactions in bold

Table 16

OLS Regression Dimension II (Individual Race) Moderator Models (N = 1062)

Independent Variables		b	Model se(b)	B
Individual Race		.07	.11	.04
Differential Association		.14	.02	.72*
(Individual Race) X (Differential Association)		-.02	.01	-.18
Intercept		-.69*	.13	
R^2	.34			
F (p < .05)	183.51			
Individual Race		.10	.13	.06
Definitions		.09	.01	.74*
(Individual Race) X (Definitions)		-.01	.01	-.17
Intercept		-.1.04*	.16	
R^2	.38			
F (p < .05)	217.68			
Individual Race		-.13	.13	-.07
Rewards		.09	.02	.40*
(Individual Race) X (Rewards)		-.02	.02	-.01
Intercept		-.21	.16	
R^2	.15			
F (p < .05)	63.87			
Individual Race		-.03	.14	-.02
Costs		.07	.02	.29*
(Individual Race) X (Costs)		-.01	.02	-.09
Intercept		-.10	.18	
R^2	.06			
F (p < .05)	20.54			

*p < .05 (one-tailed tests); significant interactions in bold

Table 17

OLS Regression Dimension II (Individual Age) Moderator Models (N = 1062)

Independent Variables		Model b	$se(b)$	B
Individual Age		.05	.02	.14*
Differential Association		.11	.04	.56*
(Individual Age) X (Differential Association)		.00	.00	-.02
Intercept		-1.25*	.31	
R^2	.35			
$F\ (p < .05)$	192.95			
Individual Age		.02	.03	.06
Definitions		.05	.02	.40*
(Individual Age) X (Definitions)		.00	.00	.21
Intercept		-1.14*	.37	
R^2	.39			
$F\ (p < .05)$	227.75			
Individual Age		.12	.03	.33*
Rewards		.13	.04	.59*
(Individual Age) X (Rewards)		-.00	.00	-.23
Intercept		-1.98*	.34	
R^2	.22			
$F\ (p < .05)$	98.27			
Individual Age		.07	.03	.19*
Costs		.00	.05	.02
(Individual Age) X (Costs)		.00	.00	.22
Intercept		-1.06*	.40	
R^2	.12			
$F\ (p < .05)$	48.62			

*$p < .05$ (one-tailed tests); significant interactions in bold

Table 18

OLS Regression Dimension III (SES [1]) Moderator Models (N = 1062)

Independent Variables	Model	
	b	$se(b)$
SES	-.06	.06
Differential Association	.12*	.01
(SES) X (Differential Association)	.01	.01
Intercept	-.61*	.04
R^2	.34	
F ($p < .05$)	180.68	
SES	-.12	.07
Definitions	.07*	.00
(SES) X (Definitions)	.01*	.00
Intercept	-.02*	.05
R^2	.38	
F ($p < .05$)	218.58	
SES	-.02	.07
Rewards	.08*	.01
(SES) X (Rewards)	.01	.01
Intercept	-.36*	.05
R^2	.15	
F ($p < .05$)	63.01	
SES	-.10	.08
Costs	.05*	.01
(SES) X (Costs)	.02	.01
Intercept	-.13*	.06
R^2	.06	
F ($p < .05$)	9.45	

*$p < .05$ (one-tailed tests); significant interactions in bold
[1] SES is a scale comprised of z-scores. Unstandardized coefficients are reported as the variables are already standardized.

Table 19

OLS Regression Dimension III (Log $_{10}$ Ethnic Heterogeneity) Moderator Models (N = 1062)

Independent Variables		Model		
		b	$se(b)$	B
Log_{10} Ethnic Heterogeneity		.10	.10	.06
Differential Association		.09	.02	.47*
(Log_{10} Ethnic Heterogeneity) X (Differential Association)		-.02	.01	-.15
Intercept		-.47*	.14	
R^2	.34			
$F (p < .05)$	179.72			
Log_{10} Ethnic Heterogeneity		.18	.13	.11
Definitions		.05	.01	.45*
(Log_{10} Ethnic Heterogeneity) X (Definitions)		-.01	.01	**-.22***
Intercept		-.69*	.17	
R^2	.38			
$F (p < .05)$	216.09			
Log_{10} Ethnic Heterogeneity		-.08	.16	-.05
Rewards		.08	.12	.38*
(Log_{10} Ethnic Heterogeneity) X (Rewards)		-.00	.02	-.00
Intercept		-.47*	.01	
R^2	.15			
$F (p < .05)$	62.09			
Log_{10} Ethnic Heterogeneity		.15	.14	.09
Costs		.01	.02	.06
(Log_{10} Ethnic Heterogeneity) X (Costs)		-.03	.02	-.22
Intercept		.07	.19	
R^2	.06			
$F (p < .05)$	20.81			

*$p < .05$ (one-tailed tests); significant interactions in bold

Table 20

OLS Regression Dimension III (Residential Mobility) Moderator Models (N = 1062)

		Model	
Independent Variables	*b*	*se (b)*	*B*
Residential Mobility	-.34	.44	-.05
Differential Association	.09	.03	.46*
(Residential Mobility) X (Differential Association)	.05	.05	.14
Intercept	-.45*	.22	
R^2	.34		
F (*p* < .05)	179.02		
Residential Mobility	.43	.53	.06
Definitions	.08	.02	.69*
(Residential Mobility) X (Definitions)	-.02	.03	-.09
Intercept	-1.13*	.26	
R^2	.38		
F (*p* < .05)	213.45		
Residential Mobility	.54	.54	.08
Rewards	.11	.03	.53*
(Residential Mobility) X (Rewards)	-.07	.06	-.17
Intercept	-.62*	.27	
R^2	.15		
F (*p* < .05)	61.16		
Residential Mobility	-1.11	.62	-.15
Costs	-.02	.04	-.07
(Residential Mobility) X (Costs)	.14	.07	.34
Intercept	.42	.31	
R^2	.05		
F (*p* < .05)	19.55		

*p < .05 (one-tailed tests); significant interactions in bold

Table 21

OLS Regression Dimension III (Family Disruption [1]) Moderator Models (N = 1062)

Independent Variables		Model	
		b	$se(b)$
Family Disruption		-.01	.05
Differential Association		.12*	.01
(Family Disruption) X (Differential Association)		-.00	.01
Intercept		-.61*	.04
R^2	.34		
F ($p < .05$)	178.97		
Family Disruption		.02	.06
Definitions		.07*	.00
(Family Disruption) X (Definitions)		-.00	.00
Intercept		-.93*	.05
R^2	.38		
F ($p < .05$)	214.82		
Family Disruption		-.02	.06
Rewards		.08*	.01
(Family Disruption) X (Rewards)		-.00	.01
Intercept		-.36*	.05
R^2	.15		
F ($p < .05$)	61.98		
Family Disruption		-.07	.07
Costs		.05*	.01
(Family Disruption) X (Costs)		.00	.01
Intercept		-.13*	.06
R^2	.05		
F ($p < .05$)	19.26		

*$p < .05$ (one-tailed tests); significant interactions in bold

[1] Family disruption is a scale comprised of z-scores. Unstandardized coefficients are reported as the variables are already standardized.

Table 22

Goodness of Fit Indices for the Social Structure-Social Learning Measurement Model (N = 1062)

Model	C^2	*df*	RMSEA	NFI	NNFI	CFI
Social Structure-Social Learning	3898.24*	100	.19	.46	.27	.46

Note. RMSEA = root root mean square error of approximation; NFI = normed fit index; NNFI = non-normed fit index; CFI = comparative fit index. Values satisfying part of the a priori criteria are in bold.

* $p < .05$

Table 23

Goodness of Fit Indices for the Differential Social Organization Measurement Model (N = 1062)

Model	C^2	df	RMSEA	NFI	NNFI	CFI
Social Structure-Social Learning	724.60*	32	.14	.75	.67	.76

Note. RMSEA = root mean square error of approximation; NFI = normed fit index; NNFI = non-normed fit index; CFI = comparative fit index. Values satisfying part of the a priori criteria are in bold.

* $p < .05$

Table 24

Goodness of Fit Indices for the Revised Differential Social Organization Measurement Model (N = 1062)

Model	C^2	*df*	RMSEA	NFI	NNFI	CFI
Social Structure-Social Learning	98.72*	24	**.05**	**.96**	**.95**	**.97**

Note. RMSEA = root mean square error of approximation; NFI = normed fit index; NNFI = non-normed fit index; CFI = comparative fit index. Values satisfying part of the a priori criteria are in bold.

* *p* < .05

Table 25

Goodness of Fit Indices for the Differential Location in the Social Structure Measurement Model (N = 1062)

Model	C^2	*df*	RMSEA	NFI	NNFI	CFI
Social Structure-Social Learning	145.95*	10	.11	**.93**	.82	.94

Note. RMSEA = root mean square error of approximation; NFI = normed fit index; NNFI = non-normed fit index; CFI = comparative fit index. Values satisfying part of the a priori criteria are in bold.

* *p* < .05

Table 26

Goodness of Fit Indices for the Theoretically Derived Structural Causes Measurement Model (N = 1062)

Model	C^2	*df*	RMSEA	NFI	NNFI	CFI
Social Structure-Social Learning	140.97*	17	.08	**.96**	**.93**	**.96**

Note. RMSEA = root mean square error of approximation; NFI = normed fit index; NNFI = non-normed fit index; CFI = comparative fit index. Values satisfying part of the a priori criteria are in bold.

* $p < .05$

Table 27

Goodness of Fit Indices for the Revised Social Structure-Social Learning Measurement Model (N = 1062)

Model	C^2	df	RMSEA	NFI	NNFI	CFI
Social Structure-Social Learning	3533.24*	85	.20	.48	.28	.49

Note. RMSEA = root mean square error of approximation; NFI = normed fit index; NNFI = non-normed fit index; CFI = comparative fit index. Values satisfying part of the a priori criteria are in bold.

* $p < .05$

Table 28

Properties of the Final Differential Social Organization, Differential Location in the Social Structure, and Theoretically Defined Structural Causes Measurement Models (N = 1062)

Constructs and Indicators	Standardized Loading	Reliability	Variance Extracted Estimate
Delinquency Construct		1.00[a]	1.00
Log_{10} Delinquency	1.00*	1.00	
Differential Social Organization Construct		.96[a]	.94
Population Density	.43	.18	
Log_{10} Race Composition	.76*	.58	
Age Composition	.62*	.38	
Near Poverty	.67*	.45	
Differential Location in the Social Structure Construct		1.00[a]	1.00
Individual Sex	1.00*	1.00	
Individual Race	1.00*	1.00	
Individual Age	1.00*	1.00	
Theoretically Defined Structural Causes Construct		.98[a]	.97
SES	.83*	.69	
Log_{10} Ethnic Heterogeneity	-.52*	.27	
Residential Mobility	-.44*	.19	
Family Disruption	-.87*	.76	
Social Learning Construct		.86[a]	.82
Differential Associations	.74*	.55	
Definitions	.92*	.85	
Rewards	.69*	.48	
Costs	.37*	.14	

Note. * $p < .05$ [a] Denotes composite reliability. The one-indicator delinquency, individual sex, individual race, and individual age variables assume no measurment error.

Table 29

Goodness-of-Fit Indices for the Social Structure-Social Learning Structural Models (N = 1062)

Model	C^2	df	RMSEA	NFI	NNFI	CFI
Differential Social Organization	2201.15*	25	.29	.22	-.13[a]	.22
Differential Location in the Social Structure	145.95*	13	.10	**.93**	.87	.94
Theoretically Defined Structural Causes	3292.47*	27	.34	0.00	-.34[a]	0.00

Note. RMSEA = root mean square error of approximation; NFI = normed fit index; NNFI = non-normed fit index;

CFI = comparative fit index. [a]The RMSEA sometimes produces values below 0 and above 1 (Hatcher, 1994). Values satisfying part of the a priori criteria are in bold.

* $p < .05$

Figure 23

Path Diagram for Social Structure-Social Learning Dimension I (Population Density), Social Learning (Differential Associations), and Delinquency

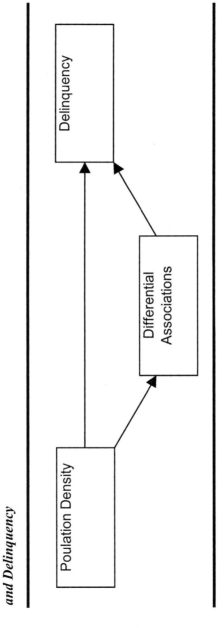

Figure 24
Social Structure-Social Learning Measurement Model

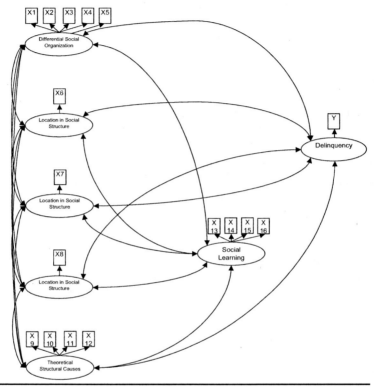

Note. Y = $\log_{10}$ delinquency. The "X" indicators correspond with the numbers in correlation Tables 8 and 9: populati race composition (X2), sex composition (X3), age composition (X4), near poverty (X5), individual sex (X6), individu age (X8), SES (X9), $\log_{10}$ ethnic heterogeneity (X10), residential mobility (X11), family disruption (X12), differentia definitions (X14), rewards (X15), and costs (X16).

Figure 25

Differential Social Organization Measurement Model

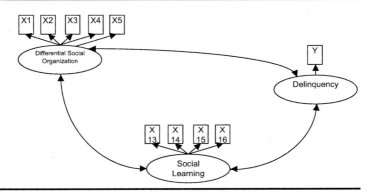

Note. Y = $\log_{10}$ delinquency. The "X" indicators correspond with the numbers in correlation T: 8 and 9: population density (X1), $\log_{10}$ race composition (X2), sex composition (X3), age comp (X4), poverty (X5), differential associations (X13), definitions (X14), rewards (X15), and costs

Figure 26

Differential Location in the Social Structure Measurement Model

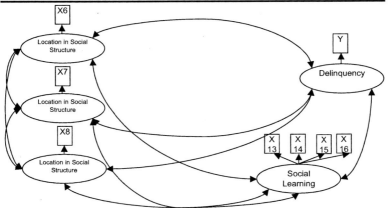

Note. Y = $\log_{10}$ delinquency. The "X" indicators correspond with the numbers in correlation T: 8 and 9: individual sex (X6), individual race (X7), individual age (X8), differential association definitions (X14), rewards (X15), and costs (X16).

Figure 27

Theoretically Derived Structural Causes Measurement Model

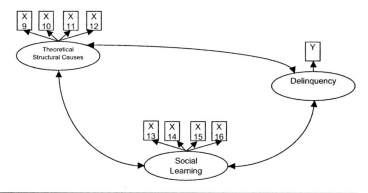

Note. $Y = \log_{10}$ delinquency. The "X" indicators correspond with the numbers in correlation Tables 8 and 9: SES (X9), $\log_{10}$ ethnic heterogeneity (X10), residential mobility (X11), family disruption (X12), differential associations (X13), definitions (X14), rewards (X15), and costs (X16).

Figure 28
Revised Social Structure-Social Learning Measurement Model

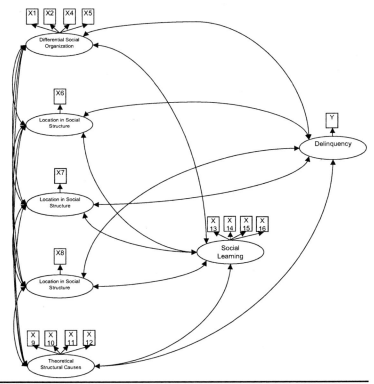

Note. Y = log$_{10}$ delinquency. The "X" indicators correspond with the numbers in correlation Tables 8 and 9: populatio log10 race composition (X2), age composition (X4), near poverty (X5), individual sex (X6), individual race (X7), indi SES (X9), log$_{10}$ ethnic heterogeneity (X10), residential mobility (X11), family disruption (X12), differential associatio definitions (X14), rewards (X15), and costs (X16).

Figure 29

Differential Social Organization Mulifactor Structural Model (N= 1062)

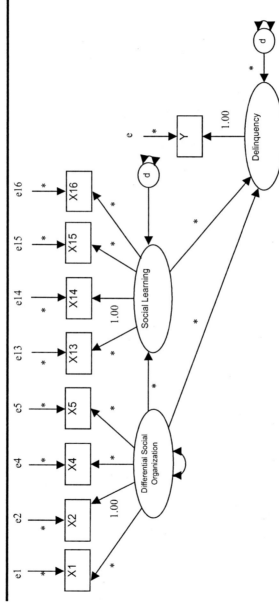

Note. An * denotes an estimated path. A "1.00" represents a fixed path. An "e" denotes variable error, and "d" represents construct error (disturbance). $Y = \log_{10}$ delinquency. The "X" indicators correspond with the numbers in correlation Tables 8 and 9: population density (X1), $\log_{10}$ race composition (X2), age composition (X4), near poverty (X5), individual sex (X6), differential associations (X13), definitions (X14), rewards (X15), and costs (X16).

Figure 30

Differential Location in the Social Structure Multifactor Structural Model (N= 1062)

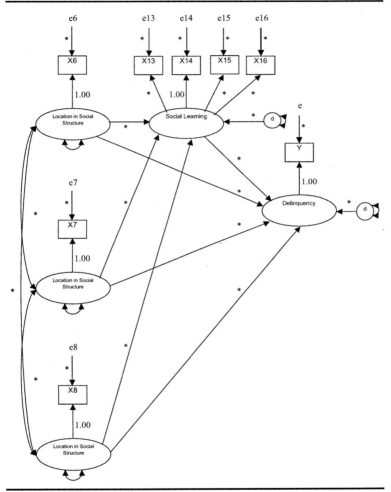

Note. An * denotes an estimated path. A "1.00" represents a fixed path. An "e" denotes variable error, an construct error (disturbance). Y = $\log_{10}$ delinquency. The "X" indicators correspond with the numbers in Tables 8 and 9: individual sex (X6), individual race (X7), individual age (X8), differential associations (X rewards (X15), and costs (X16).

Figure 31

Theoretically Defined Structural Causes Multifactor Structural Model (N = 1062)

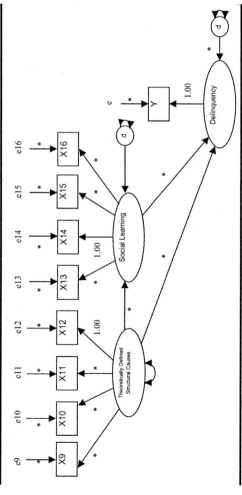

Note. An * denotes an estimated path. A "1.00" represents a fixed path. An "e" denotes variable error, and "d" represents construct error (disturbance). $Y = \log_{10}$ delinquency. The "X" indicators correspond with the numbers in correlation Tables 8 and 9: SES (X9), $\log_{10}$ ethnic heterogeneity (X10), residential mobility (X11), family disruption (X12), differential associations (X13), definitions (X14), rewards (X15), and costs (X16).

CHAPTER 6

Reconciliation of Previous Literature

SUMMARY OF THE SOCIAL STRUCTURE-SOCIAL LEARNING STATEMENT

The purpose of the present study was to test a portion of Akers' (1998) cross-level social structure-social learning model. Elaborating on social learning theory, Akers suggested that the social learning process mediates social structural effects on individual crime and deviancy. Although tests of the theory are sparse, and have limitations, they have provided a first glimpse of the effectiveness of the model.

This research sought to improve on previous research by examining the model with more complete measures of two of its social structural dimensions, and by more fully fleshing out how exactly social structure might impinge on the social learning process, areas suggested by Akers (1998, 1999) and colleagues (Lee et al., 2004) as needing more attention.

The social structure-social learning model is an elaboration of social learning theory (Akers, 1973, 1977, 1985, 1998; Burgess & Akers, 1966), which itself derived from Sutherland's (1947) differential association theory. Dissatisfied with the theoretical explanations of his time, Sutherland (1939) sought a general explanation of crime that would advance criminology as a science and provide for the meaningful control of crime. Sutherland believed that the body of science was scattered, and he sought to organize the known correlates of crime in a meaningful way (see Sutherland, 1924, 1934, 1939, 1947, 1970a, 1970b, 1970c). Sutherland first offered a tentative explanation for both crime and criminal behavior (Sutherland, 1939), before settling on his single-level theory of differential association (Sutherland, 1947).

Social learning theory addresses a major criticism of differential association theory, that it does not explicitly specify the learning mechanisms inherent in the model (Akers, 1973, 1977, 1985, 1998; Burgess & Akers, 1966). Rather than a competing explanation for deviant, delinquent, and criminal behavior, social learning theory has subsumed differential association tenets (Akers, 1998).

As a microsocial explanation for deviant behavior, social learning theory has received much empirical attention. The literature review revealed that social learning theory's concepts and variables find moderate to strong support with survey, official, cross-sectional, and longitudinal data. Further, when researchers employ theory competition, social learning theory concepts and propositions generally find more support than those derived from other simultaneously tested theories. When researchers apply social learning concepts and propositions to integrated theory, social learning variables generally have the strongest effect.

Although social learning theory offers a plausible explanation for deviant behavior, in its strictly processual form, social learning theory cannot answer why some individuals and not others encounter configurations of the social learning elements conducive to deviant behavior.

Burgess and Akers (1966) originally argued that Sutherland's (1947) supposition that learning occurs through interaction with others in social environments was compatible with the operant theory notion that environment shapes individual behavior. Burgess and Akers expounded that because differential association theory was essentially a learning theory, and that both criminal behavior and non-criminal behavior are learned through the same process, it was reasonable to incorporate modern learning knowledge into the theory. Akers' (1998) social structure-social learning elaboration emphasizes the notion that social environments shape individual behavior, and like Sutherland's (1939) original attempt to resolve perceived failings in the criminological literature, Akers (1998) tackled the task of simultaneously addressing both epidemiological and etiological explanations for crime.

Starting from a social learning framework, Akers (1998) positioned social learning theory as the proximate cause mediator of distal social structural causes of crime. Although the model has received little empirical attention, its rationale has received strong theoretical opposition. Two main critics, Sampson (1999) and Krohn (1999), collectively argue that the social structure-social learning model does not adequately specify refutable propositions linking social structure to the social learning process. Sampson rejects the model outright, finding it "uninteresting," and Krohn sees potential in the model but does not at present find it useful.

Akers (1999) responded by noting that he his less concerned with understanding the macrosocial linkages than he is with understanding crime. However, Akers' (1998) seemingly prescient remarks on the topic when explicating the model are more illuminating. Akers perhaps too subtly explained that although others were welcome to view the model as a cross-level theoretical integration, that which requires the linking of propositions, he viewed the model differently.

The social structure-social learning model that Akers (1998) presented is a cross-level, conceptual integration that following the thinking of Thornberry's (1989) theoretical elaboration, starts with the premise of social learning and expands it outward such that it becomes the process that explains macrosocial covariates of crime. The idea that drives theory elaboration is that researchers add variables to an existing theory in order to improve its adequacy (Bernard & Snipes, 1986).

Whereas theory competition (Hirschi, 1979, 1989) attempts to refute opposing theoretical expositions, and theory integration (Bernard & Snipes, 1996; Elliott et al., 1979; Liska et al., 1989) attempts to reconcile the differences, theory elaboration tries to advance science by working toward integration as if on a continuum, adding compatible concepts when applicable. Those that demand linking propositions from Akers' (1998) elaboration are not viewing it from the framework in which it was offered. They are starting from a different viewpoint than Akers, and although their position may be valid from their framework, the criteria they use to judge theory do not apply to Akers' elaboration by definition.

Substantively, Akers (1998) is presumably less concerned with linking macrosocial explanations of crime to the social learning process through propositional integration, because he views social structure generally as important to shaping the social learning process. He is not concerned with the source of that structure or any specific meaning attached to it by other theorists (see Akers, 1998, 1999).

Like Sutherland (1947), Akers (1998) views crime as rooted in societal social organization. He posits differential social organization, as well as theoretically defined structural causes such as social disorganization theory, that which was measured in the present research, and only important to Akers because others have already identified it as explaining the relationship between several correlates of crime, as cornerstones to the social structural dimensions of his social structure-social learning model. Akers views social learning as the process by which social structure influences individual criminal and deviant behavior, and consequently crime rates.

Akers (1999) believes the model is testable as it is, and that rather than more theoretical specification, it needs better empirical testing, particularly through the incorporation of good empirical and theoretically derived social structural measures (see Akers, 1999; Lee et al., 2004). Responding to Sampson (1999) and Krohn (1999), Akers did acknowledge, however, that the lack of linking propositions was the least developed portion of the theory and he invited others to help with the specification. Akers (1998) concluded his introduction to the social structure-social learning model with the comments, "I welcome others' critiques, tests, and modifications."

IMPLICATIONS OF THE PRESENT RESEARCH

Nuances of the Research Question

The argument presented in this book is that Akers (1999) correctly characterizes social structure-social learning theory (Akers, 1998) as testable, but that his insistence on conceptual rather than propositional integration is only adequate if the theory works as suggested—if social learning theory mediates the effects of social structure on crime and criminal behavior. Although the lack of linking propositions may exacerbate the interpretation of less than clear empirical findings, the present study reasoned that the theoretical adequacy of social structure-social learning theory instead more likely hinges on Akers' standard for findings that empirically support the theory, substantial rather than full statistical mediation, and his description of the process.

Akers (1998) suggests that expecting full statistical support of modeled sociological phenomena is unreasonable. Because its main premise is that social structure has no effect on individual criminal behavior, if not for its effect on the social learning process, Akers argues that an observed statistical reduction in effects supports the theory in varying degrees: weakly to fully. Akers advances the notion of substantial mediation as suitable for concluding that the theory is plausible. He loosely defines the term substantial mediation as that which is generally accepted by normal social science standards. Akers does not define the term more specifically, and the studies in the literature that have found promise for the model have used the substantial mediation standard.

The present research argued that the term substantial mediation, as well as the notion of mediation generally, requires more scrutiny than previously afforded. A review of the methodological literature suggested that although Akers may use the term mediation correctly when characterizing the process of statistically testing his model, accounting for mediational effects is more complicated than his (Lee and et al, 2004) and the other (Bellair et al., 2003; Lanza-Kaduce & Capece, 2003) two tests of the model have allowed. Because social learning variables are expected to correlate with both social structural and outcome variables, the procedure of adding social learning variables to a model that includes social structural variables, and observing the new effects, cannot discern mediation from moderation.

In such circumstances of expected correlation with the social learning variables, an incomplete mediation of effects may signal statistical mediation or statistical moderation (see Baron & Kenny, 1986). In order to conclude that mediation is plausible, researchers must first rule out moderation (see Friedrich, 1982). None of the three cited tests of social structure-social learning theory report testing the possibility of moderating effects.

Adding to the complexity, some of Akers' (e.g., 1968, 1973, 1977, 1985, 1992, 1998) characterizations of the relationship between social learning and social structure cloud the theoretical distinction between mediation and moderation. Some of Akers' characterizations seemingly describe a moderating relationship between social learning and social structure rather than a mediating relationship.

The issue is important because the idea of moderation versus mediation is essentially what distinguishes the positions of Sampson (1999), and perhaps macrosocial researchers generally, from that of Akers (1998, 1999). Akers seems to view social learning theory as the process by which social structure impacts individual behavior. If not for the intervening social learning process, social structure would have no effect on crime. Akers (1998) makes this point more obvious in his illustration of his model (p. 331), his discussion of full versus substantial mediation, and in his test of the model (Lee et al., 2004).

Sampson (1999) in contrast, which is particularly clear in his test of social disorganization theory (Sampson & Groves, 1989), views the relationship between social structure and individual behavior differently. In that test, macrosocial variables measured a structure that was antecedent to a social disorganization construct that comprised measures of community control. Social disorganization was modeled as the mediator of the same types of variables that Akers (1998) views as the distal causes of crime, through their direct effect on the social learning process.

However, Akers' (1998) model is not merely a one-for-one exchange of the social learning process with Sampson and Groves' (1989) social disorganization measure. Sampson and Groves' model serves as an explanation for crime rates, whereas Akers' model proposes that social structure influences social learning, which influences criminal behavior, which aggregate to crime rates.

When discussing Akers' (1998) social structure-social learning model, Sampson (1999) is not viewing the problem from the same perspective as Akers. Whereas Akers sees a mediation relationship between social structure and social learning, it seems more likely that Sampson sees moderation. To Sampson (Sampson & Groves, 1989), social structure serves as the antecedent cause of community control, the amount of influence various local networks are able to exert over its members, and the individual level process is presumably only important through its interaction with the predictor (social disorganization) of crime rates.

Overview of Findings

The research presented in this book tested a portion of Akers' (1998) social structure-social learning model, emphasizing broad measures of the differential social organization dimension (population density, race, sex, age, near poverty), known social structural correlates of crime, and four theoretically defined measures of social disorganization theory (SES, ethnic heterogeneity, residential mobility, family disruption). The theoretical variables derived from Sampson and Groves' (1989) test of social disorganization theory, Sun and colleagues' (2004) replication of Sampson and Groves' test using U.S. census data, and from D. Gottfredson and colleagues (1991) who identified additional important U.S. measures.

In addition to modeling the theoretical dimension more thoroughly than previous research, between the two dimensions, the study included the three concentrated disadvantage variables (racial composition, family disruption, and poverty) that Pratt and Cullen (2005) concluded must be estimated or controlled in any test of crime causes to avoid the risk of model misspecification. The study also modeled the differential location in the social structure as the mean survey sample respondent age, as well as the proportions of the respondents who were male and nonWhite.

The present research first examined the question of moderation, using OLS regression to estimate 12 models that included an interaction term for each social structure indicator and each social learning measure. At least one social structure and social learning indicator interaction was found statistically significant in each dimension. This is finding is incredibly important to both testing social structure-social learning as specified, and as a first glimpse to understanding the relationship between social learning processes and structural influences in a way different than previous research has suggested.

In the differential social organization dimension, population density statistically interacted separately with both differential associations and definitions, though in directions opposite than those hypothesized. The directions were, however, consistent with the opposite than predicted zero-order coefficient direction for population density and $\log_{10}$ delinquency.

Researchers must interpret and assess interactive models differently than standard OLS regression models because the depicted relationships are conditional rather than general (Friedrich, 1982). This is something often overlooked or done incorrectly in the literature. An interaction model measures joint impacts. The impact of one independent variable on the dependent variable depends on the level of another independent variable: The effect of the social structural variable on delinquency depends on the level of the social learning variable, and equally important, the effects of the social learning variable on delinquency depend on the level of the social structural variable.

As to the combined effects negative coefficient, the findings suggest that the impact of high population density levels on $\log_{10}$ delinquency is more substantial when the respondent reports having fewer friends that engage in delinquent behavior, or having fewer definitions favorable to self-reported delinquency (see Braumoeller, 2004). Said the other way, the results suggest that the negative impact of differential associations and definitions on delinquency is more substantial as the population density increases. Rather, having friends who skip school, steal items worth less than $50, hit to hurt, and use marijuana, or having neutralizing or lack of guilt definitions supportive of such behavior, only influences delinquency at the lower ends of population density.

The present research draws substantively similar conclusions and statements from the race composition and costs interaction term and from the age composition and differential association term. Both interaction terms produced coefficients with negative values consistent with the zero-order correlation between the social structural variable and $\log_{10}$ delinquency.

The results of the theoretically defined structural causes dimension suggest that ethnic heterogeneity (a statistically non-significant zero-order correlate of $\log_{10}$ delinquency) and definitions likewise combine to produce opposite than expected results on the delinquency measure. The SES and definitions interaction term moved in the direction anticipated, but the coefficient was trivial and SES was not a statistically significant zero-order correlate of the delinquency measure. In the differential location in the social structure dimension, sex composition statistically interacted separately with differential associations, definitions, and costs, producing statements in the anticipated directions.

Baron and Kenny (1986) remarked that results support moderation if an interactional term is statistically significant, and they advised that the statistical significance of the other two paths (e.g., population density and differential associations in the described interactional model) is irrelevant to the moderation hypothesis. Following that standard, the present research concludes that differential associations moderate rather than mediate the effects of population density, age composition, and individual sex on $\log_{10}$ delinquency; definitions moderate rather than mediate the effects of population density, individual sex, SES, and $\log_{10}$ ethnic heterogeneity on the delinquency measure; and costs moderate rather than mediate the effects of $\log_{10}$ race composition and individual sex on $\log_{10}$ delinquency.

However, Baron and Kenny (1986) also observe that when testing for moderation, a presumed moderator should ideally not correlate with either the dependent or independent variable. Social learning variables generally correlate with outcome measures, of course, and the social structure-social learning model predicts that the social learning variables will correlate with the social structure measures. Otherwise, the model would be misspecified because the theory suggests that social structure is only important to crime through its effect on the social learning process.

Such interplay between the variables does not invalidate the test of moderation, but it does cloud interpretation of significant findings (Judd & Kenny, 1981). Moreover, none of the interaction models received support for a dimension indicator across all social learning variables, nor did one social learning variable statistically interact with all macrosocial measures.

The analyses proceeded to the tests for mediation. That decision was reasoned not only by the notion that some variables had no statistically significant interactions, but further in consideration that a parsimonious SEM model would contain a social learning construct rather than the individual measures, thereby having broader measurement than the OLS regression models and the possibility of not yet known results.

Various measurement models were tested, and none of the estimated, full social structure-social learning models fit the data well. The study rejected the original and two revised models. The study also examined measurement models separately for each dimension, however, and the a priori indexes for the revised differential social organization measurement model (sex composition path set = 0) suggested that the model was a good fit with the data. Models for the other two dimensions seemed close enough to warrant further scrutiny.

The study tested three separate dimension structural models. Following the a priori goodness of fit measures strictly, the study accepted none of the models as plausible fits with the data. The study did not support Akers' (1998) mediation assertions.

Reconciliation of the Results with Previous Research

The results of the present study contradict three of the four reported tests of the social structure-social learning model (Bellair et al., 2003; Lanza-Kaduce & Capece, 2003; Lee et al, 2004; see also, Lanza-Kaduce et al., 2006). Three of the four previous tests found at least suggestive support for their mediation hypotheses. However, none of the previous tests reported testing for moderation. Moreover, the tests used various methodologies (e.g., adding an additional intervening measure into the model between social structure and social learning) and statistical tests (e.g., standardized OLS regression) that may have affected the results.

Lee and colleagues (2004) both examined the social structure-social learning model with fidelity to Akers' (1998) explication and assessed their model with a statistical technique (SEM) that is argued in this book as most appropriate for examining Akers' mediation assertions. Lee and colleagues presented the most rigorous published examination of the model to date, and it most closely compares (methodologically and statistically) to the present research. The contradictory findings warrant close examination.

Lee and colleagues (2004) estimated a full model that measured three of the four social structural dimensions and three of the four social learning variables (excluding their separate test for imitation). They measured differential social organization as a one-indicator construct: community size (rural, urban, or suburban). They measured differential location in the social structure as two one-indicator constructs, the proportion of their survey respondents who were male and the mean age of their survey respondents, and one two-indicator construct, a composite survey SES variable that measured the occupation and education of the repondents' parents. They measured differential social location in primary, secondary, and reference groups as a one-indicator construct: a continuum of whether the respondent lived in a household with no parent present, with one biological parent present, or a household with both biological parents present. Lee and colleagues did not measure the theoretically defined structural causes dimension.

Lee and colleagues (2004) measured differential peer association, definitions, and differential reinforcement consistent with the social learning literature, though they uncommonly modeled a social learning construct with the three concepts as indicators without explaining their rationale. They examined *imitation* separately because an SEM model would not converge with the measure in the equation. They drew similar substantive conclusions from the full and partial models. Referring to the overall results, Lee and colleagues commented,

> The findings of the LISREL analysis sustained the conclusion that variations in the behavioral and cognitive variables specified in the social learning process (1) account for substantial portions of the variations in adolescent use of drugs and alcohol and (2) mediate substantial, and in some instances virtually all, of the effects of gender, socio-economic status, age, family structure, and community size on these forms of adolescent deviance. (p. 29)

The findings of the present research lead to the conclusion that rather than mediate the relationship between the effects of social structure and delinquency, social learning more likely moderates the social structural effects. The present research measured social learning similarly to Lee and colleagues (2004) and although incorporating SEM as a major part of the analytic strategy, the present study did not substantiate their conclusion. In contrast, the present study seemingly refutes their finding.

The present study differed methodologically from Lee and colleagues' (2004) test in three major ways. First, the present study modeled the theoretically defined structural causes dimension that Lee and colleagues were unable to incorporate, and it included much broader measures of the social structural crime correlates dimension. Secondly, the present study estimated OLS regression interaction models, reasoning that a test of the social structure-social learning mediation statement was inappropriate unless moderation could at first be ruled out. Thirdly, the present study used different SEM model fit measures than those employed by Lee and colleagues.

The rationale behind using more complete measures of the differential social organization and theoretically defined structural causes dimension was explained earlier. If these dimensions are indeed important to the social structure-social learning model, then the disparity between Lee and colleagues' (2004) conclusions and those of the present research may be the result of misspecification of Lee and colleagues' test. They may have interpreted a model that does not adequately capture the full relationship inherent in the theoretical explanation.

The reasons why the present study tested for moderation were also explained earlier. Similar to the social structure dimensions explanation, if moderation is important to the true relationship between the social structural indicators and the social learning indicators, Lee and colleagues' (2004) tested model is misspecified, which may in part explain the discrepant results between their study and the present research.

Lastly, the rationale for why the present study used its selected a priori model fit measures, along with the reasons for the cutoff values, was also explained earlier. However, no attention was given to the goodness of fit measures used by Lee and colleagues (2004).

Following convention, Lee and colleagues (2004) reported a chi-square test statistic that suggested the model did not fit the data, but they reasoned that the indicator was not reliable in their research (also common in the methodological literature). The two indicators they relied on to conclude that the model fit the data were the goodness of fit index (GFI) and the adjusted goodness of fit index (AGFI). In the alcohol model, they reported that the GFI = .93 and the AGFI = .95. For the marijuana model, they reported that the GFI = .93 and the AGFI = .94. The imitation model for alcohol GFI was .84 and the AGFI was .53. For marijuana, the imitation GFI was .82 and the AGFI was .45. Lee and colleagues did not explain their rationale for their chosen fit measures, nor did they report their cutoff values for a good fitting model. They described the model fit in the body of the article by noting that the reported measures suggested a good fit. It is unclear if they meant that description to refer to the imitation models.

Researchers have many SEM goodness of fit measures at their disposal, and there is little agreement on which indicator is the best measure of a model's fit. One agreement in the literature tends to be the notion that using the chi-square test as the indicator of model fit tends to produce biased results. If sample size is too small, the chi-square test statistic is prone to Type I error and if sample size is too large, the statistic may lead researchers to reject a good fitting model (see Hatcher, 1994; Mulaik, James, Van Alstine, Bennett, Lind & Stilwell, 1989; Tabachnick & Fidell, 2001).

The GFI (Bentler, 1983; Joreskog & Sorbom, 1984) measures model fit by examining a weighted proportion of sample variance against an estimated covariance matrix. The idea is to produce a statistic that is analogous to the R^2 (Tanaka & Huba, 1989). Because less restricted models (estimating many data points) produce better fitting models, the AGFI adjusts the GFI based on the number of parameters that the model is required to estimate. It penalizes the model for having many parameter estimates (Mulaik et al., 1989; Tabachnick & Fidell, 2001), and thus is a conservative, presumably lower value than that of the GFI.

Generally, researchers view .90 as the cutoff for the GFI and the AGFI (Joreskog & Sorbom, 1984), and some researchers suggest no fit measure should be accepted with a value below .90 (Hu & Bentler, 1999). Hu and Bentler (1999) noted that the GFI and AGFI are sensitive to sample size, with large samples increasing the opportunity for Type I error. Although Tanaka (1987) and La Du and Tanaka (1989) found the GFI to be a good estimator in a wide range of examples, Shevlin & Miles (1998) concluded that based on a simulation study, "a cut-off value of 0.9 would result in an unacceptable number of misspecified models being accepted" (p. 85). Moreover, they concluded that any value below .95 in a model with *low factor loadings* will generally be unsatisfactory regardless of sample size.

The suitability of the GFI and AGFI as SEM goodness of fit indicators appears mixed. McDonald and Ho (2002) reveal that although the GFI and AGFI appear often in the literature, they are not the most commonly used measures. Reviewing 41 studies in the psychological literature, they found that the two most commonly reported global fit indicators were the unbiased relative fit indicator (21 studies) and the CFI (21 studies), followed by the RMSEA (20 studies). Among the other notables, the GFI was reported in 15 studies and the NNFI was reported in 13 studies.

Though the effectiveness of the GFI and AGFI is mixed in the literature, researchers tend to agree that .90 is the minimum value that should be interpreted, and that the measure is sensitive to Type I error with large sample sizes. Lee and colleagues (2004) tested models with sample sizes of 2,700 and larger, and they interpreted their imitation models with a GFI as low as .82 and an AGFI as low as .45. They interpreted their main models with a GFI as low as .93 and an AGFI as low as .94.

Lee and colleagues (2004) did not explain their reasons for interpreting the two models with fit index values below the generally ascribed .90 cutoff. They additionally did not address the issue of their reported full model AGFI values being higher than the GFI values, an illogical occurrence as the AGFI conservatively adjusts the GFI in order to penalize parameter estimation, nor did they discuss the implications of their large sample sizes, or the implications of their low factor loadings. A third explanation for the disparity between Lee and colleagues' (2004) conclusions and those of the present study may be that the GFI and AGFI main model results signify Type I error.

Nuances of the Findings

Although seemingly trying to have it both ways, hypothesizing about mediation and moderation, the present study was primarily interested in Akers' (1998) notion of mediation. The requisite to first test for moderation derived from a review of the literature. In doing so, the study was unable to accept the mediation hypotheses, and instead, several moderation hypotheses found statistical support.

Before testing the social structure-social learning model, the present research specified the hypothesized effects for the moderation and mediation models, and it also explicated a possible mechanism that links social structure to social learning: contingencies of reinforcement. Although the explicated functional relationships derived from a social structure-social learning framework, which contrasts with the relationship depicted by the moderation hypotheses, the unexpected results do not invalidate the specification of this mechanism.

It was earlier argued that social structure impinges on the social learning process through the notion of various reinforcement contingencies influencing individual reinforcement schedules. Although it was anticipated that social structure set the contingency that would otherwise not affect individual behavior if not through its impact on the social learning process, the mechanism itself is not inconsistent with a moderating relationship.

Akers (1998) and Sutherland (1939, 1947) both view crime as an expression of social organization. Such terms lend themselves to interpretation as a moderator rather than a mediator. At other times, Akers (1998) specifically describes the relationship between social learning and social structure as mediation.

The idea that social structure sets various contingencies of reinforcement that are differentially reinforced individually, allows dual characterization. The notions of contingencies of reinforcement and reinforcement schedules do not rely on the characterization of the statistical relationship between the two variables. The described linking mechanism between social structure and social learning is invariant to the mediation or moderation terminology.

The point is important because this research suggests that social structural and social learning variables *relate*, they do go together, just not in the precise way that Akers (1998) most often refers to the relationship. Although the depiction of a linking mechanism that explains the relationship between social structure and social learning at first seems incapable of being an a priori statement of the social structure-social learning model, or perhaps even not refutable as it fits both a moderating or mediating relationship, such is not the case. Recall that Akers has not fully specified his model, according to Sampson (1999), and Krohn (1999), and even Akers (1998, 1999) admits that he has made no linking propositions.

Akers (1998) sometimes refers to his model in contradictory ways. Although it was reasoned that Akers' model must be tested by SEM, in order to assess the mediational effects advanced by Akers, as opposed to HLM, which was the preferred macrosocial approach of Hoffmann (2002), and the main technique advanced by critics of Akers' theory, for example, the finding of moderating effects over mediating effects does not invalidate Akers' model. Social learning does relate to the social structural variables and their impact on delinquency. The theory predicts that, and the present research supports that assertion.

If the social learning and social structure relationship generalizes beyond this research, Akers (1998) needs to change his verbiage. As was demonstrated earlier, the literature is already full of studies that misuse the terms moderate and mediate, some in the same study, and by itself, such causes little problem for the model.

That Akers' (1998) model is not discredited by the notion of a moderating relationship instead of a mediating relationship, should that indeed be the reality, is demonstrated in part by elaboration of a point made earlier that refuted his mediation assertions. Recall the quotation that Lee and colleagues (2004) used to announce the findings of their test of the social structure-social learning model. Lee and colleagues concluded that the tested model mediated the relationship between social structure and their deviancy measures. The present research contradicted that assertion.

However, in the next paragraph, Lee and colleagues (2004) commented, "We found, as proposed by the SSSL model, that social learning theory offers a useful and empirically supported set of concepts and principles for understanding how social environmental factors have an impact on behavior (Burgess & Youngblade 1998)" (p. 29). The present research supports that finding—the well-tested and empirically supported social learning concepts moderate the impact of social structure on delinquency.

The distinction between moderation and mediation, as it turns out, does not speak to the validity of the model. However, if the present study generalizes, and if contingencies of reinforcement and reinforcement schedules adequately serve as the linking mechanism between social structure and the social learning process, the social structure-social learning statement requires modification.

Modification of the Theoretical Statement

The present research found that the combined effects of the social learning variables and indicators of the differential social organization and theoretically defined structural causes dimensions tended to impact delinquency in a direction opposite of that hypothesized. The present research suggests that the differential social organization and the theoretically defined structural causes dimension indicators combine with the social learning process to reduce delinquency. The conclusion was that social learning measures moderate the relationship of social structural variables on delinquency in an unexpected direction.

Recall the finding between differential associations and population density, for example. The model was statistically significant ($R^2 = .35$, $p < .05$), and both differential associations and the population density-differential association interaction term contributed to the model. The interaction term coefficient was negative.

Although the statistical significance of non-interaction terms is irrelevant to the moderation hypothesis (Baron & Kenny, 1986), a statistically significant contributor does have meaning (Friedrich, 1982). As the relationship between an independent and dependent variable is conditioned upon the level of another independent variable in an interaction OLS regression model, the coefficients of the non-multiplicative terms represent their independent effect on the dependent variable when the other variable is zero.

In the population density and differential associations OLS regression moderator model, the statistically significant value of the differential associations coefficient was .77. The characterization for the whole model described earlier suggested that high levels of population density and high levels of delinquent peers result in a reduction of self-reported delinquency.

The findings of the present study further suggest that although having friends who engage in delinquent behavior generally results in an increase in delinquency, as reported in the literature, it conditionally relates to self-reported delinquency only at low levels of population density. Differential associations affect delinquency equivalent to the .77 coefficient when the population density is equal to zero, thus leading to the statement that as population density increases, the effects of differential associations on delinquency reduces such that high levels of population density and high levels of differential associations reduce delinquency. The present study found similar opposite than expected characterizations for several combinations of macrosocial and individual-level interaction terms.

The findings of the present research suggest that the effects of social structure and social learning on delinquency are not constant. Moderation effects, regardless of the direction of impact, are contrary to Akers' (1998) most prominent characterization of social structure-social learning model. Moreover, social learning concepts have not previously been characterized as having conditional effects. The moderation effects suggest that in addition to the misspecification of the social structure-social learning model, the social learning model is likewise misspecified. The effects of social structure on delinquency are conditioned by the level of social learning, and the effects of social learning on delinquency are likewise conditioned by the level of various social structures.

Although such lack of constant effects is the outcome of a moderation relationship by definition, interpretation of the contingent relationship between the social structural and social learning variables may be further complicated because the social structural dimensions advanced by Akers (1998) vary in their proximity to the mechanism that operates at the individual level. Social learning variables have feedback effects generally, and Akers suggests that there is some overlap between the social learning process and the meso-level variables advanced in the social structural elaboration.

In the differential location in the social structure individual sex and differential associations moderator model, for example, the statistically significant interaction term moved in the direction expected. Elaborate explanation is not needed. The interaction of maleness and differential associations combine to increase $\log_{10}$ delinquency. In this dimension, some other process appears to be going on than that of the differential social organization or theoretically defined structural causes dimensions, which interacted with social learning variables to reduce delinquency.

To understand the differential location in social structure dimension, it is important to remember that its indicators do not represent broad social structures, rather they represent an aggregate of the individual sample characteristics. Individual sex is the proportion of respondents in the sample who are male.

The differential location in the social structure dimension described by Akers (1998) seems to represent a meso-level structure. It seems more in line with the differential social location in primary, secondary, and reference groups dimension, that which provides the immediate context for larger groupings, than the implied structures of the differential social organization or theoretically defined structural causes dimensions. Being around a small group of males, for example, may provide the opportunity for translating the messages of a larger grouping of males.

The findings of the present study lead to the conclusion that the social learning process may moderate social structural variables that represent the differential social organization and theoretically defined structural causes dimensions in such a way that the combined effects reduce rather than increase delinquency. The study further suggests that these dimensions represent more distal causes of crime than variables that represent the differential location in the social structure dimension, as well as the differential social location in primary, secondary, and reference groups, which was not modeled in the present study.

Further, the present study suggests that the social learning process might interact with differential location in the social structure indicators in such a way that the combined effects increase the propensity of delinquency. However, the interpretations presents in this book recognize that this dimension also closely resembled a mediator relationship in the SEM models, if not for the stringent a priori fit measures. Although its structural model was rejected in the present research, the model would have found support with the less stringent measures utilized by Lee and colleagues (2004). Although only the NFI suggested support for a mediational relationship in the present research, the GFI (.97) and AGFI (.91) met the standards used by Lee and colleagues.

One possible explanation for this apparent discrepancy stems from the notion of moderated mediation (James & Brett, 1984). When testing interaction, it is ideal that the suspected moderators not correlate with independent or dependent variables (Baron & Kenny, 1986). In the present research, social learning variables correlate with both social structural and delinquency variables. The moderation interpretation was not clean.

As moderated mediation is possible, the question becomes, how might social learning variables act both as a moderator and as a mediator of social structural variables? If the present study's tested models are not misspecified, the alternative is that Akers' (1998) social structure-social learning theoretical model is misspecified. Social learning serves as both a moderator and a mediator of social structural variables because the model does not account for some unknown relationship. If variables do indeed operate as both a moderator and a mediator of social structure, then Akers is not describing the process correctly.

An argument presented in this book is that reinforcement contingencies and reinforcement schedules possibly form the mechanism that links social structure to the social learning process. Also, recall Figure 4, or the bottom model in Figure 5, path diagrams that show social structure indirectly influencing delinquency through the social learning process. If the findings of Lee and colleagues (2004) are correct, Akers' (1998) model finds support. If the moderator models of the present study are correct, the first reaction is to presume that the Lee and colleagues, and thus Akers', mediation model is incorrect. However, social structural reinforcement contingencies and individual reinforcement schedules may interact in such a way that portions of both the moderator and mediator hypotheses are correct.

It was presented earlier that social structure may set reinforcement contingencies that are reinforced at the individual level differentially. The process of reinforcement and extinction was offered as a possible explanation for the aging out effect, for example. So described, reinforcement contingencies and reinforcement schedules are a dichotomy that equate to the structural and individual levels.

Akers' (1998) social structure-social learning model, in contrast, does not present a dichotomy between social structure and individual behavior so much as it presents a continuum of social structure, which was thought to impact individual behavior, and crime rates, only through the social learning process. Differential social location in the primary, secondary, and reference groups, along with differential location in the social structure represent the proximate interpretation of more distal structures such as those empirically or theoretically derived.

If Akers' (1998) social structure-social learning is conceptualized more as a dichotomy, the question becomes not how does social structure impinge on the social learning process, but rather how are reinforcement contingencies, which are produced from the social structure, transmitted to reinforcement schedules, which occur at the individual level? One possible framework is that the transmittal process occurs through the small groups that actually reinforce or punish behavior. As such, social learning-social structure is not comprised of two empirical and theoretical dimensions and two smaller-group dimensions, rather it more logically comprises one distal (macro-level) dimension and one more proximate (meso-level) dimension.

Rather than social learning mediating the social structural effects on delinquency, distal macrosocial correlates of crime may influence criminal behavior through their interaction with the social learning process, whereas more proximate meso-level crime correlates may provide the messages social learning mediates. This explanation accounts for both the moderation effects observed in the present research and for the mediation effects noted in the literature (Bellair et al., 2003; Lanza-Kaduce & Capece, 2003; Lee, et al., 2004).

Relating the interpretation of the present study's results to the Lanza-Kaduce and Capece (2003) findings is straightforward. They, like Lee and colleagues (2004) did not measure strong macrosocial indicators, instead modeling measures that the present study views as meso-level. Their findings relate to the present study in similar fashion to the findings of Lee and colleagues.

As to Bellair and colleagues (2003), their findings require more interpretation to relate to the present research. They used theoretically derived measures of concentrated disadvantage similar to those used in the present research. They concluded that the concentrated disadvantage measures had no relationship with social learning or delinquency, but that other social structural effects on the outcome measure were mediated upon introducing social learning variables to the equation, along with a family well-being construct.

Bellair and colleagues (2003) added an additional construct to the model than that posited by Akers (1998), and it was this family well-being construct, combined with its direct effect on social learning variables, which mainly mediated the effects of occupational structure. They modified Akers' model using the rationale that the new construct comprised of family income and family structure (single parent household) helped translate the contextual messages offered in the broader social structure.

In essence, though not describing it as such, Bellair and colleagues (2003) measured Akers' (1998) differential social location in primary, secondary and reference groups dimension, as indexed by Lee and colleagues (2004), and placed it between social structure and the social learning process as a mediator. Consequently, their finding that the family well-being and social learning measures mediated the impact of their social structure measures on their outcome measure is consistent with the conclusion drawn from the present research. The present research characterizes the family well-being variables as the meso-level structure that affects delinquency through the mediation of social learning.

Although Bellair and colleagues (2003) modeled what the present research considers a meso-level variable as a mediator of social structure's effects on criminal behavior, rather than social learning as specified by Akers (1998) and adopted by the present research, their model is nonetheless consistent with the present study's description of the functional relationships because the differential social location in primary, secondary, and reference groups dimension overlaps with the social learning process. In specifying the dimension, Akers qualified his statements by noting that the meso-level dimension may be difficult to distinguish from the individual level social learning process.

Lastly, this study's interpretation of ambiguous data (Sampson, 1999) is also consistent with the main conclusions drawn by Sampson and Groves (1989) in their test of social disorganization theory. They found that local community control mediated the effects of their social structure measures (indexed in a similar way in the present research) on their outcome measures.

Sampson and Groves (1989) describe and measure local community control in a manner that is similar to the social structure-social learning dimension of differential location in primary, secondary, and reference groups. When viewing Akers' (1998) social structure-social learning model as a macro-level and meso-level dichotomy, Sampson and Groves' intervening construct equates to the role of the meso-level dimension in the modified social structure-social learning model. Moreover, recall that Veysey and Messner (1999), upon reexamining Sampson and Groves' model with SEM, concluded that Sampson and Groves' intervening mechanism comprised more than one dimension, one of which, they concluded, was a social learning construct.

One explanation for how social structure-social learning (Akers, 1998) might mediate crime at the meso-level, yet interact at the more distal macrosocial level to reduce crime might stem from Wirth's (1938) characterization of urbanism. Recall that he considered large cities as a place of superficial relations.

Using the present research findings that population density and differential associations interact to reduce delinquency as an example, large communities might represent a place where individuals not only have little in common, but may also tend to know lots of people in a superficial way. In the Largo sample, respondents in the areas with higher populations may know many people in a superficial way, may characterize the relationship as friendship, because such superficial interaction is normal, yet the individual may not be influenced by the individuals they have identified as friends that engage in delinquent behavior.

Such a characterization holds less for the race composition, age composition, and ethnic heterogeneity interactions, particularly for those interactions that included social learning concepts other than differential associations, such as the costs measure. However, the functional relationships between social structure and social learning may nonetheless be consistent with macrosocial literature.

Whereas Wirth (1938) anticipates social stratification from urbanicity to be represented by race and age, as well as high population density, and for such social structure to take on the characteristics he describes as inherent in large, densely populated areas, Park and Burgess (1925) characterize the inner-workings of the urban communities differently than Wirth. Instead of being unconstrained by superficial urban relations, as suggested by Wirth, Park and Burgess suggested that urban neighborhoods provide a sense of community.

In the community depiction, high levels of stratification based on social structures such as race, age, sex, and poverty might create opportunities for stronger interpersonal relationships rather than weaker interactions. This depiction follows the notion of community social control depicted earlier in the discussions of Shaw and McKay (1942, 1969), Sampson and Groves (1989), and the like. Rather than allowing greater anonymity, high levels of race and age composition and ethnic heterogeneity, important in the present research, might combine with high levels of social learning variables to reduce delinquency because contrary small group social learning processes may be overridden by strong community structures that provide ample opportunity for reinforcement contingencies that reward conformity.

The conclusions from the present research are that the functional relationship between macrosocial contingencies of reinforcement, microsocial reinforcement schedules, and delinquency includes the notion that individuals seek opportunities for social reinforcement. The interplay between macrosocial structure and the meso-level groups that actually reward or punish behavior might be most noticeable in areas that are socially stratified.

In such areas, the macrosocial contingencies of reinforcement, more normally distal, and bearing weaker messages than the more proximate structures that translate the messages into rewards or punishment, may take on the same role as the meso-level structures. Areas of high stratification may have higher area cohesiveness that influences individual behavior similar to the ways otherwise shaped by small group networks. Such highly stratified areas may get the message to individual behavior directly, without the translation from smaller group networks. Individuals might still receive messages from smaller groups that are conducive to law violation, but as the larger community messages are cohesive, and amply rewarding, or punishing, the messages of conformity are acted upon—in this way, high levels of structural stratification might interact with high levels of deviant social learning processes to reduce rather than increase delinquency.

CHAPTER 7

Future Research

LIMITATONS OF THE PRESENT RESEARCH

The present research has several limitations. The first pertains to generalizability. Although the micro-level data comprise a random sample of students in the select schools, the study does not purport to generalize beyond the schools. Particularly, the research may not generalize to youth less protected than those attending school (see discussion of street criminology versus school criminology in Hagan and McCarthy, 1998).

A second limitation has to do with scope. Like much of the social learning literature, the present study focused on minor forms of delinquency.

The remaining limitations have to do with methodology. Skew and kurtosis were present in several variables, and the study relied on several transformations to normalize the data. Study analyses assume normality, multivariate normality in the case of SEM, and the implications of nonnormality in these data mainly represent misinterpretation of the inferential procedures. Although there is much literature to suggest that the analyses used in the present study are robust to assumptions of normality, the literature is mixed on some points.

Further, the possibility of misinterpretation may have been exacerbated by the selection of strict model fit criteria in the SEM analyses, particularly in respect to the CFI. Many researchers use .90 as a cutoff, but the present research specified the CFI value according to the more conservative views of Hu and Bentler (1998, 1999), who suggest .95 or higher as an indicator of a good model fit. This decision made the difference between the final SEM structural model having one out of four indexes suggest a good fit instead of two out of the four.

However, because the study set four fit measures a priori, the final model would have been rejected regardless. Moreover, the moderator analyses, also subject to the possibility of error stemming from nonnormal data (for an explanation of why concerns of multicollinearity distorting coefficients in interactive regression are warrantless see Friedrich, 1982), further suggested that mediation was not how the variables interrelated. Despite the possibility of biased coefficients in the SEM analyses, the moderator results suggest that the substantive conclusions would not have differed.

Lastly there is the issue of relative model fit. The literature offers a wide range of SEM measures by which to judge a model's fit. The rationale for selecting the specific measures and their cutoff points was explained earlier.

However, the variety of measures exist, in part, because of a lack of consensus over what type of support is actually needed to be assured of a reasonable fit, and because of the growing dissatisfaction with the chi-square statistic's stringency on requiring a perfect fit (see Hatcher, 1994). The various measures intentionally relax certain criteria in order to find an approximate fit. Measures that start with an "r" tend to model relative fit, like the RMSEA in the present research, and the NFI and NNFI are designed to be more in line with the purpose of the chi-square statistic, accounting for its tendency to underestimate in small samples and overestimate in large samples (see Hatcher, 1994).

Researchers that use .90 as a cutoff for the NFI, NNFI, and the CFI, as well as those who use .95 for the CFI, tend to qualify their lower limit by suggesting that the closer to 1.00 the better (e.g., Bentler, 1989; Hu & Bentler, 1999). What is not addressed in the literature is whether a model that falls below the cutoff is "almost there," such as might be suggested considering that there seems to be a scale between .90-1.00, or whether the model should be rejected outright such as what was done in the present research, following the rationale used in OLS regression that a non-significant model is not interpreted, no matter how close the *p*-value. Strict adherence to a priori indicators of hypothesis plausibility is what drives the scientific processes, and the present study argues that as the research was not exploratory, instead testing a theory, such formal hypothesis testing procedures were mandated.

CONCLUDING REMARKS

The present research sought to test Akers' (1998) assertion that social learning theory mediates social structural influences on delinquency. The study utilized the three measures (race poverty, and family disruption) that Pratt and Cullen (2005) identified in a macro-level predictors meta-analysis as "among the strongest and most stable predictors " (p. 373) of crime. Further, the study measured social disorganization theory variables in a manner similar to that used by Sampson (Sampson & Groves, 1989), one of the social structure-social learning model's more vocal skeptics (Sampson, 1999).

Secondly, this book introduced possible linkages between social structure and the social learning process in an attempt to address the concerns of Krohn (1999), who suggested that the theory does not adequately do so, and Sampson (1999), who suggested that the theory is incapable of producing a priori, refutable macrosocial propositions. Further, the present research critically examined Akers' (1998) notion that social learning mediates the relationship between social structure and crime, introducing the possibility that social learning may instead moderate social structure's effect on crime and criminal behavior.

This book presented the argument that clarifying this distinction may contribute to understanding how exactly social structure might influence the social learning process. Combined, the two aims of this book, utilizing more complete social structural measures and explaining how social structure might impinge on the social learning process, responded to Akers' (1999) plea to help specify the most underdeveloped portion of the model.

Although finding a relationship between social structure and social learning, the present research suggested no support for Akers' (1998) description of the relationship as mediation. The study instead found support for several moderator hypotheses, concluding that Akers' model requires modification.

Reconciling the discrepancies of the present research with previous tests of Akers' (1998) model, this book explored a theoretical argument that links social structure to social learning through the mechanisms of macrosocial reinforcement contingencies. The book presented the argument that such an explanation accounts for the findings in the present research (moderation) and the findings in the literature (mediation). The present research led to a reconceptualization of the model such that social structure is viewed as influencing individual behavior by sets of reinforcement contingencies that are transmitted to the social learning process through meso-level groups.

The implications of the present research suggest that future research should focus on distinguishing macrosocial structures from meso-level groups most likely to have the most impact on the social learning process. Although the findings presented in this book suggest that macrosocial structure interacts with social learning to affect delinquency, suggesting that social learning mediates the effects of meso-level structure on individual delinquency, the arguments presented here offer that the mechanisms by which these structures impinge on individual behavior, macrosocial reinforcement contingencies influencing individual reinforcement schedules, might work dichotomously. The present research suggests that the proximity of the social structural contingencies of reinforcement in relation to the translating macro-level structures is important, and that this distinction needs attention in future tests of the model.

References

Akers, R.L. (1968). Problems in the sociology of deviance: Social definitions and behavior. *Social Forces, 46*(4), 455-465.

Akers, R.L. (1973). *Deviant behavior: A social learning approach.* Belmont, CA: Wadsworth Publishing Company.

Akers, R.L. (1977). *Deviant behavior: A social learning approach* (2nd ed). Belmont, CA: Wadsworth Publishing Company.

Akers, R.L. (1985). *Deviant behavior: A social learning approach* (3rd ed). Belmont, CA: Wadsworth Publishing Company.

Akers, R.L. (1989). *A social behaviorist's perspective on integration of theories of crime and deviance.* In S.F. Messner, M.D. Krohn, & A.E. Liska (Eds.), Theoretical integration in the study of deviance and crime (pp. 23-36). Albany, NY: State University of New York Press.

Akers, R.L. (1990). Rational choice, deterrence, and social learning theory in criminology: The path not taken. *Journal of Criminal Law and Criminology, 81*(3), 653-676.

Akers, R.L. (1992). *Drugs, alcohol, and society: Social structure, process, and policy.* Belmont, CA: Wadsworth Publishing Company.

Akers, R.L. (1998). *Social learning and social structure: A general theory of crime and deviance.* Boston: Northeastern University Press.

Akers, R.L. (1999). Social learning and social structure: Reply to Sampson, Morash, and Krohn. *Theoretical Criminology, 3*(4), 477-493.

Akers, R.L., & Cochran, J.K. (1985). Adolescent marijuana use: A test of three theories of deviant behavior. *Deviant Behavior, 6*, 323-346.

Akers, R.L., & La Greca, A.J. (1991). *Alcohol use among the elderly: Social learning, community context, and life events.* In D.J. Pittman, & H.R. White (Eds.), Society, culture, and drinking patterns re-examined (pp. 242-262). New Brunswick, NJ: Rutgers Center of Alcohol Studies.

Akers, R.L., & Lee, G. (1996). A longitudinal test of social learning theory: Adolescent smoking. *Journal of Drug Issues, 26*(2), 317-343.

Akers, R.L., & Lee, G. (1999). Age, social learning, and social bonding in adolescent substance use. Deviant Behavior, 20(1), 1-25.

Akers, R.L., & Sellers, C.S. (2004). Criminological theories: Introduction, evaluation, and application (4th ed.). Los Angeles: Roxbury.

Akers, R.L., Krohn, M.D., Lanza-Kaduce, L., & Radosevich, M. (1979). Social learning and deviant behavior: A specific test of a general theory. American Sociological Review, 44, 636-655.

Akers, R.L., La Greca, A.J., Cochran, J.K., & Sellers, C.S. (1989). Social learning theory and alcohol behavior among the elderly. Sociological Quarterly, 30, 625-638.

Alarid, L.F., Burton, V.S., Jr., & Cullen, F.T. (2000). Gender and crime among felony offenders: Assessing the generality of social control and differential association theories. Journal of Research in Crime and Delinquency, 37(2), 171-199.

Allen, M., Donohue, W.A., Griffin, A., Ryan, D., & Mitchell-Turner, M.M. (2003). Comparing the influence of parents and peers on the choice to use drug: A meta-analytic summary of the literature. Criminal Justice and Behavior, 30(2), 163-186.

Allison, J.P. (1972). Economic factors and the rate of crime. Land Economics, 48, 193-196.

American Psychological Association [APA]. (1992). Ethical principles of psychologists. Washington, DC: American Psychological Association.

Anderman, C., Cheadle, A., Curry, S. Diehr, P., Shultz, L., & Wagner, E. (1995). Selection bias related to parental consent in school-based survey research. Evaluation Review, 19, 663-674.

Anderson, J.C., & Gerbing, D.W. (1988). Structural equation modeling in practice: A review and recommended two-step approach. Psychological Bulletin, 103(3), 411-423.

Archer, D., Gartner, R., Akert, R., & Lockwood, T. (1978). Cities and homicide: A new look at an old paradox. Comparative studies in sociology, 1, 73-95.

Arnold, H.J. (1982). Moderator variables: A clarification of conceptual, analytic, and psychometric issues. Organizational Behavior and Human Performance, 29, 143-174.

Arnold, H.J. (1984). Testing moderator variable hypotheses: A reply to Stone and Hollenbeck. Organizational Behavior and Human Performance, 34, 214-224.

Asher, H.B. (1988). Causal modeling (2nd ed.). Beverly Hills, CA: Sage.

Bailey, W.C. (1984). Poverty, inequality, and city homicide rates. Criminology, 22, 531-550.

Bailey, W.C. (1999). The socioeconomic status of women and patterns of forcible rape for major U.S. cities. Sociological Focus, 32, 43-63.

Ball, J.C. (1957). Delinquent and Non-delinquent attitudes toward the prevalence of stealing. Journal of Criminal Law, Criminology, and Police Science, 48, 259-274.

Bandura, A. (1977). Social learning theory. Englewood Cliffs, NJ: Prentice-Hall, Inc.

Baron, R.M., & Kenny, D.A. (1986). The moderator-mediator variable distinction in social psychological research: Conceptual, strategic, and statistical considerations. Journal of Personality and Social Psychology, 51(6), 1173-1182.

Baum, S. (1999). An aggregate level analysis of the socioeconomic correlates of drink driving offenders. Accident analysis and prevention, 31, 213-220.

Bauman, K.E., Foshee, V.A., Linzer, M.A., & Koch, G.G. (1990). Effect of parental smoking on the association between parental and adolescent smoking. Addictive Behaviors, 15, 413-422.

Bellair, P.E. (1997). Social interaction and community crime: Examining the importance of neighbor networks. Criminology, 35, 677-703.

Bellair, P.E., Roscigno, V.J., & Vélez, M.B. (2003). Occupational structure, social learning, and adolescent violence. In R.L. Akers, & G.F. Jensen (Eds.), Social learning theory and the explanation of crime: A guide for the new century, volume 11 advances in criminological theory (pp. 197-225). New Brunswick, NJ: Transaction Publishers.

Benda, B.B. (1994). Testing competing theoretical concepts: Adolescent alcohol consumption. Deviant Behavior, 15, 375-396.

Benda, B.B., & Corwyn, R.F. (2002). The effect of abuse in childhood and in adolescence on violence among adolescents. Youth and Society, 33(3), 339-365.

Bentler, P.M. (1983). Some contributions to efficient statistics in structural models: Specifications and estimation of moment structures. Psychometrika, 48, 493-517.

Bentler, P.M. (1989). EQS structural equations program manual. Los Angeles: BMDP Statistical Software.

Bentler, P.M., & Bonett, D.G. (1980). Significance tests and goodness-of-fit in the analysis of covariance structures. Psychological Bulletin, 88, 588-606.

Bentler, P.M., & Chou, C.P. (1987). Practical issues in structural modeling. Sociological Methods and Research, 16(1), 78-117.

Bergesen, A., & Herman, M. (1998). Immigration, race, and riot: The 1992 Los Angeles uprising. American Sociological Review, 63, 39-54.

Bernard, T.J. (1990). Twenty years of testing theories. Journal of Research in Crime and Delinquency, 24(4), 325-347.

Bernard, T.J. (2001). Integrating theories in criminology. In R. Paternoster & R. Bachman (Eds.), Essays in contemporary criminological theory: Explaining criminals and crime (pp. 335-346). Los Angeles: Roxbury Publishing.

Bernard, T.J., & Ritti, R. (1990). The role of theory in scientific research. In K. Kempf (Ed.), Measurement issues in criminology (pp. 1-20). New York: Springer-Verlag.

Bernard, T.J., & Snipes, J.B. (1996). Theoretical integration in criminology. In M. Tonry (Ed.), Crime and justice: A review of the research, volume 20 (pp. 301-348). Chicago: University of Chicago Press.

Blalock, H.M. (1984). Contextual-effects models: Theoretical and methodological issues. Annual Review of Sociology, 10(2), 353-372.

Blau, P.M. (1960). Structural effects. American Sociological Review, 25(2), 178-193.

Blau, P.M. (1977). Inequality and heterogeneity: A primitive theory of social structure. New York: Free Press.

Blau, J., & Blau, P.M. (1982). The cost of inequality: Metropolitan structure and violent crime. American Sociological Review, 47, 114-129.

Bollen, K.A. (1989). Structural equations with latent variables. New York: Wiley.

Bollen, K.A., & Paxton, P. (1998). Interactions of latent variables in structural equation models. Structural Equation Modeling, 5, 267-293.

Brady, D. (2003). Rethinking the sociological measurement of poverty. Social Forces, 81(3), 715-752.

Braithwaite, J. (1989). Crime, shame, and reintegration. New York: Cambridge University Press.

Braumoeller, B.F. (2004). Hypothesis testing and multiplicative interaction terms. International Organization, 58(4), 807-820.

Brick, J.M., & Kalton, G. (1996). Handling missing data in survey research. Statistical Methods in Medical Research, 5, 215-238.

Browne, M.W. (1984). Asymptotically distribution-free methods for analysis of covariance structures. British Journal of Mathematical and Statistical Psychology, 37, 62-83.

Brownfield, D., & Thompson, K. (2002). Distinguishing the effects of peer delinquency and gang membership on self-reported delinquency. Journal of Gang Research, 9(2), 1-10.

Bryk, A., & Raudenbush, S.W. (1992). Hierarchical linear models for social and behavioral research: Applications and data analysis methods. Newbury Park, CA: Sage.

Burgess, R.L., & Akers, R.L. (1966). A differential association-reinforcement theory of criminal behavior. Social Forces, 14, 128-147.

Bursik, R.J., Jr., (1988). Social disorganization and theories of crime and delinquency: Problems and prospects. Criminology, 26(4), 519-551.

Bursik, R.J., Jr., & Grasmick, H.G. (1992). Longitudinal neighborhood profiles in delinquency: The decomposition of change. Journal of Quantitative Criminology, 8, 247-263.

Bursik, R.J., Jr., & Grasmick, H.G. (1993). Neighborhoods and crime: The dimensions of the effective community control. New York: Lexington Books.

Bursik, R.J., Jr., & Grasmick, H.G. (1996). The use of contextual analysis in models of criminal behavior. In J.D. Hawkins (Ed.), Delinquency and crime: Current theories (pp. 236-267). New York: Cambridge University Press.

Bursik, R.J., & Webb, J. (1982). Community change and patterns of delinquency. American Journal of Sociology, 88, 24-42.

Burton, V., Cullen, F., Evans, D., & Dunaway, R.G. (1994). Reconsidering strain theory: Operationalization, rival theories, and adult criminality. Journal of Quantitative Criminology, 10, 213-239.

Byrne, J.M. (1986). Cities, citizens, and crime: The ecological/nonecological debate reconsidered. In R.J Sampson & J.M. Byrne (Eds.), The social ecology of crime (pp.77-101). New York: Springer-Verlag.

Byrne, J.M., & Sampson, R.J. (1986). Key issues in the social ecology of crime. In R.J Sampson & J.M. Byrne (Eds.), The social ecology of crime (pp.1-22). New York: Springer-Verlag.

Cameron, A.C., & Trivedi, P.K. (1998). Regression analysis of count data. New York: Cambridge University Press.

Chamlin, M.B. (1989). Conflict theory and police killings. Deviant Behavior, 10, 353-368.

Chappell, A.T., & Piquero, A.R. (2004). Applying social learning theory to police misconduct. *Deviant Behavior, 25*(2), 89-108.

Chiricos, T.G. (1987). Rates of crime and unemployment: An analysis of aggregate research evidence. Social Problems, 34, 187-212.

Chunrong, A., & Norton, E.C. (2003). Interaction terms in logit and probit models. Economic Letters, 80, 123-129.

Cleary, P.D., & Kessler, R.C. (1982). The estimation and interpretation of modified effects. Journal of Health and Social Behavior, 23, 159-169.

Cloward, R.A. (1959). Illegitimate means, anomie, and deviant behavior. American Sociological Review, 24(2), 164-176.

Cohen, A.K. (1962). Multiple factor approaches. In M.E. Wolfgang, L. Savitz, & N. Johnston (Eds.), The sociology of crime and delinquency (pp.77-80). New York: John Wiley.

Cohen, J., & Cohen, P. (1983). Applied multiple regression/correlation analysis for the behavioral sciences (2nd ed.). Hillside, NJ: Erlbaum.

Cohen, L.E., & Land, K.C. (1987). Age structure and crime: Symmetry versus asymmetry and the projection of crime rates through the 1990s. American Sociological Review, 52, 170-183.

Comrey, A.L. (1978). Common methodological problems in factor analysis studies. Journal of Consulting and Clinical Psychology, 46, 648-659.

Conger, R.D. (1976). Social control and social learning models of delinquent behavior: A synthesis. Criminology, 14(1), 17-40.

Conway, K.P., & McCord, J. (2002). A longitudinal examination of the relation between co-offending with violent accomplices and violent crime. Aggressive Behavior, 28, 97-108.

Conway, R.W., & McClain, J.O. (2003). The conduct of an effective simulation study. Transactions on Education, 3(3), 13-2.

Copes, H. (1999). Routine activities and motor vehicle theft: A crime specific approach. Journal of Crime and Justice, 22, 125-146.

Cortina, J.M. (1993). What is coefficient alpha? An examination of theory and applications. Journal of Applied Psychology, 78(1), 98-104.

Cressey, D.R. (1960). Epidemiology and individual conduct: A case from criminology. The Pacific Sociological Review, 3(2), 47-58.

Cronbach, L.J. (1951). Coefficient alpha and the internal structure of tests. Psychometrika, 16(3), 297-334.

Cronbach, L.J. (1976). Research on classrooms and schools: Formulation of questions, design and analysis. Stanford, CA: Stanford University Evaluation Consortium.

Crutchfield, R.D., Garken, M.R., & Grove, W.R. (1982). Crime rates and social integration: The impact of metropolitan mobility. Criminology, 20, 467-478.

Curran, P.J., West, S.G., & Finch, J.F. (1996). The robustness of test statistics to nonnormality and specification error in confirmatory factor analysis. Psychological Methods, 1(1), 16-29).

Curry, G.D., & Spergel, I.A. (1988). Gang homicide, delinquency, and community. Criminology, 26, 381-405.

Davis, J.A., Spaeth, J.L., & Huson, C. (1961). A technique for analyzing the effects of group composition. American Sociological Review, 26(2), 215-225.

DeCarlo, L.T. (1997). On the meaning of kurtosis. Psychological Methods, 2(3), 292-307.

DeMaris, A. (2004). Regression with social data: Modeling continuous and limited response variables. Hoboken, NJ: Wiley & Sons.

Dembo, R., Grandon, G., La Voie, L., Schmeidler, J., & Burgos, W. (1986). Parents and drugs revisited: Some further evidence in support of social learning theory. Criminology, 24(1), 85-104.

Dewey, J. (1931). Social science and social control. New Republic, 67, 276-277.

Diez-Roux, A.V. (1998). Bringing context back into epidemiology: Variables and fallacies in multilevel analysis. American Journal of Public Health, 88, (2), 588-594.

Diez-Roux, A.V. (2003). A glossary for multilevel analysis. Journal of Epidemiology and Community Health, 56, 588-594.

Durkheim. E. (2002). Suicide. In K. Thompson (Ed.), Readings from Emile Durkheim (pp. 91-115). New York: Routledge. (Original work published 1897)

Elliott, D.S. (1985). The assumption that theories can be combined with increased explanatory power. In R.F. Meier (Ed.), Theoretical methods in criminology (pp. 123-149). Beverly Hills, CA: Sage.

Elliott, D.S., Ageton, S.S., & Cantor, R.J. (1979). An integrated theoretical perspective on delinquent behavior. Journal of Research in Crime and Delinquency, 16(1), 3-27.

Elliott, D.S., Huizinga, D., & Ageton, S.S. (1985). Explaining delinquency and drug use. Beverly Hills, CA: Sage Publications.

Elliott, D.S., & Menard, S. (1996). Delinquent friends and delinquent behavior: Temporal and developmental patterns. In J.D. Hawkins (Ed.), Delinquency and crime: Current theories (pp. 28-67). New York: Cambridge University Press.

Erickson, M.L. & Jensen, G.F. (1997). Delinquency is still group behavior: Toward revitalizing the group premise in the sociology of deviance. Journal of Criminal Law and Criminology, 88, 262-273.

Fan, X., & Wang, L. (1998). Effects of potential confounding factors on fit indices and parameter estimates for true and misspecified models. Structural Equation Modeling, 5, 701-735.

Farnworth, M. (1989). Theory integration versus model building. In S.F. Messner, M.D. Krohn, & A.E. Liska (Eds.), Theoretical integration in the study of deviance and crime (pp. 93-100). Albany, NY: State University of New York Press.

Farrell, A.D., & Danish, S.J. (1993). Peer drug associations and emotional restraint: Causes or consequences of adolescents' drug use? Journal of Consulting and Clinical Psychology, 61(2), 327-334.

Farrington, D.P., Loeber, R., Stouthamer-Loeber, M., Van Kammen, W.R., & Schmidt, L. (1996). Self-reported delinquency and a combined delinquency seriousness scale based on boys, mothers, and teachers: Concurrent and predictive validity for African-Americans and Caucasians. Criminology, 34(4), 493-517.

Ferster, C.B., & Skinner, B.F. (1957). *Schedules of reinforcement.* Acton, MA: Copley Publishing Group.

Finch, J.F., West, S.G., & MacKinnon, D.P. (1997). Effects of sample size and nonnormality on the estimation of mediated effects in latent variable models. Structural Equation Modeling, 2, 87-105.

Findley, M.J., & Cooper, H.M. (1983). Locus of control and academic achievement: A literature review. Journal of Personality and Social Psychology, 44, 419-427.

Fleisher, B.M. (1966). The effect of income on delinquency. American Economic Review, 56, 118-137.

Flom, P.L., Friedman, S.R., Kottiri, B.J., Neaigus, A., & Curtis, R. (2001). Recalled adolescent peer norms towards drug use in young adulthood in a low-income, minority urban neighborhood. Journal of Drug Issues, 31(2), 425-443.

Florida Department of Education. (2003). Florida school indicators report [Data file]. Available at http://www.fldoe.org

Florida Department of Law Enforcement. (1999). Crimes and crime rates statistics [Data file]. Available at http://fl.rand.org/cgi-bin/annual.cgi

Ford, J.K., MacCallum, R.C., & Tait, M. (1986). The application of exploratory factor analysis in applied psychology: A critical review and analysis. Personnel Psychology, 39, 291-314.

Franzblau, A.N. (1958). A primer of statistics for non-statisticians. New York: Harcourt, Brace, and World.

Friedrich, R.J. (1982). The workshop: In defense of multiplicative terms in multiple regression equations. American Journal of Political Science, 26(4), 797-833.

Galtung, J. (1969). Theories and methods of social research. New York: Columbia University Press.

Gardner, W., Mulvey, E.P., & Shaw, E.S. (1995). Regression analyses of counts and rates: Poisson, overdispersed Poisson, and negative binomial models. Psychological Bulletin, 118(3), 392-404.

Gartner, R., Baker, K., & Pampel, F.C. (1990). Gender stratification and the gender gap in homicide victimization. Social Problems, 37, 593-612.

Gauthier, D.K., & Bankston, W.B. (1997). Gender equality and the sex ratio of intimate killing. Criminology, 35, 577-600.

Gibbs, J.P. (1972). Sociological theory construction. Hinsdale, IL: Dryden Press.

Gibbs, J.P., & Erickson, M.L. (1976). Crime rates of American cities in ecological context. American Journal of Sociology, 82, 605-620.

Glaser, D. (1954). A reconsideration of some parole prediction factors. American Sociological Review, 19, 335-351.

Glaser, D. (1960). Differential association and criminological prediction. Social Problems, 8, 6-14.

Glaser, D., & Rice, K. (1959). Crime, age, and employment. American Sociological Review, 24(5), 679-686.

Glueck, S. (1956). Theory and fact in criminology. British Journal of Delinquency, 7, 92-109.

Glueck, S., & Glueck, E. (1950). Unraveling juvenile delinquency. Cambridge, MA: Harvard University Press.

Gold, M. (1970). Delinquent behavior in an American city. Belmont, CA: Wadsworth.

Gordon, D.M. (1972). Theories of poverty and underemployment: Orthodox, radical, and dual market perspectives. Lexington, MA: Lexington Books.

Gottfredson, D., McNeil, R.J., & Gottfredson, G.D. (1991). Social area influences on delinquency: A multilevel analysis. Journal of Research in Crime and Delinquency, 28(2), 197-226.

Gottfredson, M.R., & Hirschi, T. (1987). The methodological adequacy of longitudinal research on crime. Criminology, 25(3), 581-614.

Gottfredson, M.R., & Hirschi, T. (1990). A general theory of crime. Stanford, CA: Stanford University Press.

Greenberg, D.E. (1985). Age, crime, and social explanation. American Journal of Sociology, 91, 1-12.

Guadagnoli, S.W., & Velicer, W. (1988). Relation of sample size to the stability of component patterns. Psychological Bulletin, 103, 265-275.

Hagan, J., & McCarthy, B. (1998). Mean streets: Youth crime and homelessness. NY: Cambridge University Press.

Hagenaars, A.J.M. (1991). The definition and measurement of poverty. In L. Osberg (Ed.), Economic inequality and poverty: International perspectives (pp. 134-156). Armonk, New York: M.E. Sharpe.

Hair, J.F., Jr., Anderson, R.E., Tatham, R.L., & Black, W.C. (1998). Multivariate data analysis (5th ed.). Upper Saddle River, NJ: Prentice Hall.

Hamblin, R.L. (1979). Behavioral choice and social reinforcement: Step function versus matching. Social Forces, 57(4), 1141-1156.

Hannan, M.T. (1971). Aggregation and disaggregations in sociology. Lexington, MA: Heath-Lexington.

Hannan, M.T. (1985). Problems of aggregation. In H.M. Blalock, Jr. (Ed.), Causal models in the social sciences (2nd ed.) (pp. 403-439). New York: Aldine.

Harkins, S.G., Latane, B., & Williams, K. (1980). Social loafing: Allocating effort or taking it easy? Journal of Experimental Social Psychology, 16, 457-465.

Hartung, F.E. (1965). Crime, law, and society. Detroit, MI: Wayne State University Press.

Hatcher, L. (1994). A step-by-step approach to using the SAS system for factor analysis and structural equation modeling. Cary, NC: SAS Institute.

Hauser, R.M. (1970). Context and consex: A cautionary tale. American Journal of Sociology, 75(4, Part 2), 645-664.

Haynie, D.L. (2002). Friendship networks and delinquency: The relative nature of peer delinquency. Journal of Quantitative Criminology, 18(2), 99-134.

Heitgard, J.L., & Bursik, R.J. (1987). Extracommunity dynamics and the ecology of delinquency. American Journal of Sociology, 92, 775-787.

Herrnstein, R.J. (1974). Formal properties of the matching law. Journal of the Experimental Analysis of Behavior, 21, 159-164.

Herrnstein, R.J., & Loveland, D.H. (1975). Maximizing and matching on concurrent ratio schedules. Journal of the Experimental Analysis of Behavior, 24, 107-116.

Higgins, G.E., Fell, B.D., & Wilson, A.L. (2006). Digital piracy: Assessing the contributions of an integrated self. *Criminal Justice Studies, 19*(1), 3-22.

Hinduja, S. (2006). *Music piracy and crime theory:* New York: LFB Scholarly.

Hinkle, D.E., Wiersma, W., & Jurs, S.G. (1988). Applied statistics for the behavioral sciences (2nd. ed.). Boston: Houghton Mifflin.

Hirschi, T. (1969). Causes of delinquency. Berkeley, CA: University of California Press.

Hirschi, T. (1979). Separate but unequal is better. Journal of Research in Crime and Delinquency, 16 (1), 34-38.

Hirschi, T. (1989). Exploring alternatives to integrated theory. In S.F. Messner, M.D. Krohn, & A.E. Liska (Eds.), Theoretical integration in the study of deviance and crime (pp. 37-49). Albany, NY: State University of New York Press.

Hirschi, T., & Gottfredson, M. (1983). Age and the explanation crime. American Journal of Sociology, 89, 553-584.

Hirschi, T., & Selvin, H.C. (1967). Delinquency research: An appraisal of analytic methods. New York: Free Press.

Hoffmann, J.P. (2002). A contextual analysis of differential association, social control, and strain theories of delinquency. Social Forces, 81(3), 753-785.

Holland, J.G., & Skinner, B.F. (1961). *The analysis of behavior: A program for self-instruction.* New York: McGraw-Hill.

Holmbeck, G. N. (1997). Toward terminological, conceptual, and statistical clarity in the study of mediators and moderators: Examples from the child-clinical and pediatric psychology literatures. Journal of Consulting and Clinical Psychology, 65(4), 599-610.

Hox, J.J., & Kreft, I.G.G. (1994). Multilevel analysis methods. Sociological Methods and Research, 22(3), 283-299.

Hu, L., & Bentler, P.M. (1998). Fit indices in covariance structure modeling: Sensitivity to underparameterized model misspecification. *Psychological Methods, 3*(4), 424-453.

Hu, L., & Bentler, P.M. (1999). Cutoff criteria for fit indexes in covariance structure analysis: Conventional criteria versus new alternatives. *Structural Equation Modeling, 6*(1), 1-55.

Huizinga, D., &Elliott, D.S. (1986). Reassessing the reliability and validity of self-report delinquency measures. *Journal of Quantitative Criminology, 2,* 293-327.

Huizinga, D., Esbensen, F.A., & Weiher, A.W, (1991). Are there multiple paths to delinquency? *Journal of Criminal Law and Criminology, 82*, 83-118.

Hwang, S., & Akers, R.L. (2006). Parental and peer influences on adolescent drug use in Korea. *Asian Journal of Criminology, 1*(1), 51-69.

Iannotti, R.J., & Bush, P.J. (1992). Perceived vs. actual friends' use of alcohol, cigarettes, marijuana, and cocaine: Which has the most influence? *Journal of Youth and Adolescence, 21*, 375-389.

Jaccard, J., & Wan, C.K. (1995). Measurement error in the analysis of interaction effects between continuous predictors using multiple regression: Multiple indicator and structural equation approaches. Psychological Bulletin, 117(2), 348-357.

Jaccard, J., & Wan, C.K. (1996). LISREL approaches to interaction effects in multiple regression. Thousand Oaks, CA: Sage.

Jackson, P.I. (1984). Opportunities and crime: A function of city size. Sociology and Social Research, 68, 173-193.

James, L.R., & Brett, J.M. (1984). Mediators, moderators, and tests for mediation. Journal of Applied Psychology, 69(2), 307-321.

Jang, S.J. (1999). Age-varying effects of family, school, and peers on delinquency: A multilevel modeling test of interactional theory. Criminology, 37(3), 643-696

Jang, S.J. (2002). The effects of family, school, peers, and attitudes on adolescents' drug use: Do they vary with age? Justice Quarterly, 19(1), 97-127.

Jaquith, S.M. (1981). Adolescent marijuana and alcohol use: An empirical test of differential association theory. Criminology, 19(2), 271-280.

Jeffery, C.R. (1965). Criminal behavior and learning theory. The Journal of Criminal Law, Criminology and Police Science, 56(3), 294-300.

Jessor, R., Jessor, S.L., & Finney, J. (1973). A social psychology of marijuana use: Longitudinal studies of high school and college youth. Journal of Personality and Social Psychology, 26, 1-15.

Johnson, R.E., Marcos, A.C., & Bahr, S.J. (1987). The role of peers in the complex etiology of adolescent drug use. Criminology, 25(2), 324-339.

Johnson, V. (1988). Adolescent alcohol and marijuana use: A longitudinal assessment of a social learning perspective. American Journal of Drug and Alcohol Abuse, 14, 419-439.

Johnstone, J.W.C. (1978). Social class, social areas and delinquency. Sociology and Social Research, 63, 49-77.

Joreskog, K.G., & Sorbom, D. (1984). LISREL VI. Mooresville, IN: Scientific Software, Inc.

Joreskog, K.G., & Sorbom, D. (1989). LISREL 7: A guide to the program and applications (2nd ed.). Chicago: SPSS Inc.

Joreskog, K.G., & Yang, F. (1996). Nonlinear structural equation models: The Kenny-Judd model with interaction effects. In G.A. Marcoulides, & R.E. Schumacker (Eds.), Advanced structural equation modeling: Issues and techniques (p. 239-250). Mahwah, NJ: Erlbaum.

Judd, C.M., & Kenny, D.A. (1981). Estimating the effects of social interventions. New York: Cambridge University Press.

Judd, C.M., Kenny, D.A., & McClelland, G.H. (2001). Estimating and testing mediation and moderation in within-subject designs. Psychological Methods, 6(2), 115-134.

Julian, M.W. (2001). The consequences of ignoring multilevel data structures in nonhierarchical covariance modeling. Structural Equation Modeling, 8(3), 325-352.

Kaiser, H.F. (1960). The application of electronic computers to factor analysis. Educational and Psychological Measurement, 20, 141-151.

Kalton, G., & Kasprzyk, D. (1986). The treatment of missing survey data. Survey Methodology, 12(1), 1-16.

Kandel, D.B. (1996). The parental and peer contexts of adolescent deviance: An algebra of interpersonal influences. Journal of Drug Issues, 26, 289-315.

Kandel, D.B., & Andrews, K. (1987). Process of adolescent socialization by parents and peers. International Journal of the Addictions, 22, 319-342.

Kandel, D.B., & Davies, M. (1991). Friendship networks, intimacy, and illicit drug use in young adulthood: A comparison of two competing theories. Criminology, 29(3), 441-470.

Kaplan, D. (2000). Structural equation modeling: Foundations and extensions. Thousand Oaks, CA: Sage.

Kaplan, H.B., Martin, S.S., & Robbins, C. (1984). Pathways to adolescent drug use: Self-derogation, peer influence, weakening of social controls, and early substance use. Journal of Health and Social Behavior, 25, 270-289.

Kapuskinski, C.A., Braithwaite, J., & Chapman, B. (1998). Unemployment and crime: Toward resolving the paradox. Journal of Quantitative Criminology, 14, 215-244.

Kasarda, J.D., & Janowitz, M. (1974). Community attachment in mass society. American Sociological Review, 39(3), 328-339.

Kempf, K.L. (1993). The empirical status of Hirschi's control theory. In F. Adler and W.S. Laufer (Eds.), New directions in criminological theory, volume 4 advances in criminological theory (pp. 143-185). New Brunswick, NJ: Transaction Publishers.

King, G. (1988). Statistical models for political science event counts: Bias in conventional procedures and evidence for the exponential Poisson regression model. American Journal of Political Science, 32, 838-863.

King, D.W., & King, L.A. (1997). A brief introduction to structural equation modeling. PTSD Research Quarterly, 8(4), 1-4.

Klein, A., & Moosbrugger, H. (2000). Maximum likelihood estimation of latent interaction effects with the LMS method. Psychometrika, 65, 457-474.

Kline, R.B. (1998). Principles and practices of structural equation modeling. New York: Guilford Press.

Kline, R.B. (2005). Principles and practices of structural equation modeling (2nd ed.). New York: Guilford Press.

Kornhauser, R.R. (1978). Social sources of delinquency: An appraisal of analytic models. Chicago: University of Chicago Press.

Kraemer, H.C., Stice, E., Kazdin, A., Offord, D., & Kupfer, D. (2001). How do risk factors work together? Mediators, moderators, and independent, overlapping, and proxy risk factors. American Journal of Psychiatry, 158(6), 848-856.

Kreft, I.G.G. (1996). Are multilevel techniques necessary? An overview, including simulation studies [on-line]. Los Angeles, CA; California State University. Available at http://www.calstatela.edu/faculty/ikreft/quarterly/quarterly.html

Kreft, I., & de Leeuw, J. (1998). Introducing multilevel modeling. Thousand Oaks, CA: Sage.

Krivo, L.J., & Peterson, R.D. (1996). Extremely disadvantaged neighborhoods and urban crime. Social Forces, 75, 619-650.

Krohn, M.D. (1986). The web of conformity: A network approach to the explanation of delinquent behavior. Social Problems, 33(6), 81-93.

Krohn, M.D. (1999). Social learning theory: The continuing development of a perspective. Theoretical Criminology, 3(4), 462-476.

Krohn, M.D., Lanza-Kaduce, L., & Akers, R.L. (1984). Community context and theories of deviant behavior: An examination of social learning and social bonding theories. Sociological Quarterly, 25, 353-372.

Krohn, M.D., Lizotte, A.J., Thornberry, T.P., Smith, C., & McDowall, D. (1996). Reciprocal causal relationships among drug use, peers, and beliefs: A five-wave panel model. Journal of Drug Issues, 26, 405-428.

Krohn, M.D., Skinner, W.F., Massey, J.L., & Akers, R.L. (1985). Social learning theory and adolescent cigarette smoking: A longitudinal study. Social Problems, 32, 455-473.

Krull, J.L., & MacKinnon, D.P. (2001). Multilevel modeling of individual and group level mediated effects. Multivariate Behavioral Research, 36(2), 249-277.

La Du, T.J., & Tanaka, J.S. (1989). The influence of sample size, estimation method, and model specification on goodness-of-fit assessments in structural equation models. *Journal of Applied Psychology, 71*, 625-636.

Lakatos, I. (1978). *The methodology of scientific research programmes*. London, UK: Cambridge University Press.

Land, K.C., McCall, P.L., & Cohen, L.E. (1990). Structural covariates of homicide rates: Are there any invariances across time and social space? *American Journal of Sociology, 95*(4), 922-963.

Lanza-Kaduce, L., & Capece. M. (2003). *Social structure-social learning (SSSL) and binge drinking: A specific test of an integrated theory*. In R.L. Akers and G. F. Jensen (Eds.), Social learning theory and the explanation of crime: A guide for the new century, volume 11 advances in criminological theory (pp. 179-196). New Brunswick, NJ: Transaction Publishers.

Lanza-Kaduce, L., & Klug, M. (1986). Learning to cheat: The interaction of moral-development and social learning theories. *Deviant Behavior, 7*, 243-259.

Lanza-Kaduce, L., Akers, R.L., Krohn, M.D., & Radosevich, M. (1982). Conceptual and analytical models in testing social learning theory: Reply to Stafford and Ekland-Olson and Strickland. *American Sociological Deviant Behavior, 5*, 79-96.

Lanza-Kaduce, L., Capece, M., & Alden, H. (2006). *Liquor is quicker: Gender and social learning among college students. Criminal Justice Policy Review, 17*(2), 127-143.

Lanza-Kaduce, L., Akers, R.L., Krohn, M.D., & Radosevich, M. (1984). Cessation of alcohol and drug use among adolescents: A social learning model. *American Sociological Review, 47*(1), 169-173.

Largo Chamber of Commerce. (1998). *Largo demographics* [Data file]. Available at http://www.largochamber.com

Lazarsfeld, P.F., & Menzel, H. (1961). *On the relation between individual and collective properties.* In A. Etzioni (Ed.), Complex organizations (pp. 422-440). New York: Rinehart & Winston.

Lei, M., & Lomax, R.G. (2005). The effect of varying degrees of nonnormality in structural equation modeling. *Structural Equation Modeling, 12*(1), 1-27.

Lee, G., Akers, R.L., & Borg, M.J. (2004). Social learning and structural factors in adolescent substance use. Western Criminology Review, 5(1), 17-34.

Lewis, D.A., & Salem, G. (1981). Community crime prevention: An analysis of a developing strategy. Crime and Delinquency, 27, 405-421.

Lewis, C.J., Sims, L.S., & Shannon, B. (1989). Examination of specific nutrition/health behaviors using a social cognitive model. Journal of the American Dietetic Association, 89(2), 194-202.

Lindesmith, A.R. (1938). A sociological theory of drug addiction. American Journal of Sociology, 43, 593-613.

Liska, A.E. (1969). Uses and misuses of tautologies in social psychology. Sociometry, 32(4), 444-457.

Liska, A.E., Krohn, M.D., & Messner, S.F. (1989). Strategies and requisites for theoretical integration in the study of crime and deviance. In S.F. Messner, M.D. Krohn, & A.E. Liska (Eds.),

Theoretical integration in the study of deviance and crime (pp. 1-20). Albany, NY: State University of New York Press.

Liska, A.E., Logan, J.R., & Bellair, P.E. (1998). Race and violent crime in the suburbs. American Sociological Review, 63, 27-38.

Loehlin, J.C. (1992). Latent variable models: An introduction to factor, path, and structural analysis (2nd ed.). Hillsdale, NJ: Lawrence Erlbaum.

Loftin, C., & Hill, R.H. (1974). Regional subculture and homicide: An examination of the Gastil-Hackney thesis. American Sociological Review, 39, 714-724.

Long, J.S. (1997). Regression models for categorical and limited dependent variables. Thousand Oaks, CA: Sage.

Lowenkamp, C.T., Cullen, F.T., & Pratt, T.C. (2003). Replicating Sampson and Groves's test of social disorganization theory: Revisiting a criminological classic. Journal of Research in Crime and Delinquency, 40(4), 351-373.

MacKinnon, D.P., Lockwood, C.M., Hoffman, J.M., West, S.G., & Sheets, V. (2002). A comparison of methods to test mediation and other intervening variable effects. Psychological Methods, 7(1), 83-104.

Marcos, A.C., Bahr, S.J., & Johnson, R.E. (1986). Test of a bonding/association theory of adolescent drug use. Social Forces, 65(1), 135-161.

Mardia, K.V., Kent, J.T., & Bibby, J.M. (1979). Multivariate analysis. New York: Academic.

Matsueda, R.L. (1988). The current state of differential association theory. Crime & Delinquency, 34(3), 277-306.

Matsueda, R.L., & Anderson, K. (1998). The dynamics of delinquent peers and delinquent behavior. Criminology, 36(2), 269-308.

Matsueda, R.L., & Heimer, K. (1987). Race, family structure, and delinquency: A test of differential association and social control theories. American Sociological Review, 52, 826-840.

Maly, M.T. (2000). The neighborhood diversity index: A complementary measure of racial residential settlement. Journal of Urban Affairs, 22(1), 37-47.

McDonald, R.P., Ho, M.R. (2002). Principles and practice in reporting structural equation analyses. Psychological Methods, 7(1), 64-82.

McKay, H.D. (1960). Differential association and crime prevention: Problems of utilization. Social Problems, 8(1), 25-37).

Mead, G.H. (1934). Mind, self, and society. Chicago: University of Chicago Press.

Mencken, F.C., & Barnett, C. (1999). Murder, nonnegligent manslaughter, and spatial autocorrelation in mid-South counties. Journal of Quantitative Criminology, 15, 407-422.

Messner, S.F. (1982). Poverty, inequality, and the urban homicide rate. Criminology, 20, 1030115.

Messner, S.F., & Sampson, R.J. (1991). The sex ratio, family disruption, and rates of violent crime. Social Forces, 69(3), 693-713.

Michaels, J.W., & Miethe, T.D. (1989). Applying theories of deviance to academic cheating. Social Science Quarterly, 70(4), 870-885.

Miethe, T.D., Hughes, M., & McDowall, D. (1991). Social change and crime rates: An evaluation of alternative theoretical approaches. Social Forces, 70, 165-185.

Mladenka, K.R., & Hill, K.Q. (1976). A reexamination of the etiology of urban crime. Criminology, 13, 491-506.

Moffitt, T.E. (1993). Adolescence-limited and life-course-persistent antisocial behavior: A developmental taxonomy. Psychological Review, 100(4). 674-701.

Morenoff, J.D., & Sampson, R.J. (1997). Violent crime and the spatial dynamics of neighborhood transition: Chicago, 1970-1990. Social Forces, 76, 31-64.

Mulaik, S.A. (1987). A brief history of the philosophical foundations of exploratory factor analysis. Multivariate Behavioral Research, 22, 267-305.

Mulaik, S.A., James, L.R., Van Alstine, J., Bennett, N., Lind, S., & Stilwell, C.D. (1989). Evaluation of goodness-of-fit indices for structural equation models. Psychological Bulletin, 105(3), 430-445.

Muthen, B.O. (1989). Latent variable modeling in heterogeneous populations. Psychometrika, 54, 557-85.

Muthen, B., & Kaplan, D. (1992). A comparison of some methodologies for the factor analysis of non-normal Likert variables: A note on the size of the model. British Journal of Mathematical and Statistical Psychology, 45, 19-30.

Myers, D. (1992). Analysis with local census data: Portraits of change. San Diego, CA: Academic Press.

Neapolitan, J.L. (1998). Cross-national variation in homicides: Is race a factor? Criminology, 36, 139-156.

Neff, J.L., & Waite, D.E. (2007). Male versus female substance abuse patterns among incarcerated juvenile offenders: Comparing strain and social learning variables. *Justice Quarterly, 24*(1), 106-132.

Nunnally, J.C. (1978). Psychometric theory (2nd ed.). New York: McGraw-Hill.

O'Brien, R.M. (1991). Sex ratios and rape rates: A power control theory. Criminology, 29, 99-114.

Oberwittler, D. (2004). A multilevel analysis of neighborhood contextual effects on serious juvenile offending. European Journal of Criminology, 1(2), 201-235.

Oetting, E.R., & Beauvais, F. (1987). Common elements in youth drug abuse: Peer clusters and other psychosocial factors. Journal of Drug Issues, 2, 133-151.

Olsson, U.H., Foss, T., Troye, S.V., & Howell, R.D. (2000). The performance of ML, GLS, and WLS estimation in structural equation modeling under conditions of misspecification and nonnormality. Structural Equation Modeling, 7, 557-595.

Osborn, D.R., Trickett, A., & Elder, R. (1992). Area characteristics and regional variates as determinants of area property crime levels. Journal of Quantitative Criminology, 8, 265-285.

Osgood, D.W. (2000). Poisson-based regression analysis of aggregate crime rates. Journal of Quantitative Criminology, 16(1), 21-43.

Osgood, D.W., & Anderson, A.L. (2004). Unstructured socializing and rates of delinquency. Criminology, 42(3), 519-549.

Park, R.E., & Burgess, W. (1925). The city. Chicago: University of Chicago press.

Patterson, E.B. (1991). Poverty, income inequality, and community crime rates. Criminology, 29, 755-776.

Patterson, G.R., & Dishion, T.J. (1985). Contributions of families and peers to delinquency. Criminology, 23(1), 63-79.

Pearson, F.S., & Weiner, N.A. (1985). Toward an integration of criminological theories. Journal of Criminal Law and Criminology, 76(1), 116-150.

Peeples, F., & Loeber, R. (1994). Do individual factors and neighborhood context explain ethnic differences in juvenile delinquency? Journal of Quantitative Criminology, 10(2),141-157.

Peterson, R.A. (2000). A meta-analysis of variance accounted for and factor loadings in exploratory factor analysis. Marketing Letters, 11(3), 261-275.

Peterson, R.D., & Bailey, W.C. (1988). Forcible rape, poverty, and economic inequality in U.S. metropolitan communities. Journal of Quantitative Criminology, 4, 99-119.

Philips, L., & Votey, H.L. (1972). Crime, youth, and the labor market. Journal of Political Economy, 80, 491-504.

Ping, R.A. (1996). Latent variable interaction and quadratic effect estimation: A two-step technique using structural equation analysis. Psychological Bulletin, 119, 166-175.

Piquero, A.R., MacIntosh, R., & Hickman, M. (2002). The validity of a self-reported delinquency scale: Comparisons across gender, age, race, and place of residence. Sociological Methods and Research, 30(4), 492-529.

Pokorny, S.B., Jason, L.A., Schoeny, M.E., Townsend, S.M., & Curie, C.J. (2001). Do participation rates change when active consent procedures replace passive consent? Evaluation Review, 25(5), 567-580.

Popper, K. (2002). The logic of scientific discovery (6th ed.). New York: Routledge.

Pratt, T.C., & Cullen, F.T. (2005). Assessing macro-level predictors and theories of crime: A meta-analysis. Crime and Justice, 32, 373-450.

Pressman, I., & Carol, A. (1971). Crime as diseconomy of scale. Review of Social Economy, 19, 227-236.

Quetelet, A. (1984). Research on the propensity for crime at different ages. (S. Sylvester, trans.). Cincinnati, OH: Anderson. (Original work published 1831)

Raudenbush, S., Bryk, A., Cheong, Y.F., & Congdon, R. (2001). Hierarchical linear and nonlinear modeling. Lincolnwood, IL: Scientific Software International.

Raykov, T., & Marcoulides, G.A. (2000). A first course in structural equation modeling. Mahwah, NJ: Lawrence Erlbaum.

Rebellon, C.J. (2002). Reconsidering the broken homes/delinquency relationship and exploring its mediating mechanism(s). Criminology, 40(1), 103-136.

Regnerus, M.D. (2002). Friends' influence on adolescent theft and minor delinquency: A developmental test of peer-reported effects. Social Science Research, 31, 681-705.

Reiss, A.J., Jr. (1951). Delinquency as the failure of personal and social controls. American Sociological Review, 16, 196-208.

Reiss, A.J., Jr., & Rhodes, A.L. (1961). The distribution of juvenile delinquency in the social class structure. American Sociological Review, 26, 720-732.

Reiss, A.J., Jr., & Rhodes, A.L. (1964). An empirical test of differential association theory. Journal of Research in Crime and Delinquency, 1, 5-18.

Riedel, M. (2000). Research strategies for secondary data: A perspective for criminology and criminal justice. Thousand Oaks, CA: Sage.

Robbins, L.N. (1974). Deviant children grown up: A sociological and psychiatric study of sociopathic personality. Huntington, NY: R.E. Krieger.

Robinson, W.S. (1950). Ecological correlations and the behavior of individuals. American Sociological Review, 15(3), 351-357.

Roncek, D.W., & Maier, P.A. (1991). Bars, blocks, and crimes revisited: Linking the theory of routine activities to the empiricism of hot spots. Criminology, 29, 725-755.

Rountree, P.W., Land, K.C., & Miethe. T.D. (1994). Macro-micro integration in the study of victimization: A hierarchical logistic model analysis across Seattle Neighborhoods. Criminology, 32(3), 387-414.

Rozeboom, W.W. (1956). Mediation variables in scientific theory. Psychological Review, 63, 249-264.

Sampson, R.J. (1985). Structural sources of variation in race-age-specific rates of offending across major U.S. cities. Criminology, 23(4), 647-673.

Sampson, R.J. (1986). Neighborhood family structure and the risk of personal victimization. In R.J. Sampson and J.M. Byrne (Eds.), The social ecology of crime (pp. 25-46). New York: Springer-Verlag.

Sampson, R.J. (1987). Urban Black violence: The effect of male joblessness and family disruption. American Journal of Sociology, 93, 348-382.

Sampson, R.J. (1988). Local friendship ties and community attachment in mass society: A multilevel systemic model. American Sociological Review, 53, 766-779.

Sampson, R.J. (1999). Techniques of research neutralization. Theoretical Criminology, 3(4), 438-450.

Sampson, R.J., & Groves, W.B. (1989). Community structure and crime: Testing social-disorganization theory. American Journal of Sociology, 94(4), 774-802.

Sampson, R.J., & Laub, J.H. (1993). Crime in the making: Pathways and turning points through life, Cambridge, MA: Harvard University Press.

Sampson, R.J., & Raudenbush, S.W. (1999). Systematic observation of public spaces: A new look at disorder in urban neighborhoods. American Journal of Sociology, 105, 603-651.

Sampson, R.J., Raudenbush, S.W., & Earls, F. (1997). Neighborhoods and violent crime: A multilevel study of collective efficacy. Science, 277(5328), 918-924.

SAS Institute. (1999). SAS/STAT user's guide (8th ed.). Cary, NC: SAS Institute.

Saunders, D.R. (1956). Moderator variables in prediction. Educational and Psychological Measurement, 16, 209-222.

Sellers, C.S., Cochran, J.K., & Winfree, T.L., Jr. (2003). Social learning theory and courtship violence: An empirical test. In R.L. Akers and G. F. Jensen (Eds.), Social learning theory and the explanation of crime: A guide for the new century, volume 11 advances in criminological theory (pp. 109-129). New Brunswick, NJ: Transaction Publishers.

Sellers, C.S., & Winfree, T.L., Jr. (1990). Differential associations and definitions: A panel study of youthful drinking behavior. International Journal of the Addictions, 25, 755-771.

Sellin, T. (1938). Culture conflict and crime: A report of the subcommittee on delinquency of the committee on personality and culture. New York: Social Science Research Council.

Shaw, C.R., & McKay, H. (1942). Juvenile delinquency and urban areas: A study of rates of delinquency in relation to differential characteristics of local communities in American Cities. Chicago: University of Chicago Press.

Shaw, C.R., & McKay, H. (1969). Juvenile delinquency and urban areas: A study of rates of delinquency in relation to differential

characteristics of local communities in American Cities (2nd ed.).
Chicago: University of Chicago Press.

Shaw, C.R., Zorbaugh, F.M., McKay, H.D. & Cottrell, L.S. (1929).
Delinquency areas: A study of the geographic distribution of
school truants, juvenile delinquents, and adult offenders in
Chicago. Chicago: The University of Chicago Press.

Shevlin, M., & Miles, J.N.V. (1998). Effects of sample size, model
specification and factor loadings on the GFI in confirmatory factor
analysis. Personality and Individual Differences, 25, 85-90.

Short, J.F., Jr. (1957). Differential association and delinquency. Social
Problems, 4, 233-239.

Short, J.F., Jr. (1958). Differential association with delinquent friends
and delinquent behavior. Pacific Sociological Review, 1, 20-24.

Short, J.F., Jr. (1960). Differential association as a hypothesis:
Problems of empirical testing. Social Problems, 8, 14-24.

Shrout, P.E., & Bolger, N. (2002). Mediation in experimental and
Nonexperimental studies: New procedures and recommendations.
Psychological Methods, 7(4), 422-445.

Silver, E., & Miller, L.L. (2004). Sources of informal social control in
Chicago neighborhoods. Criminology, 42(3), 551-583.

Simcha-Fagan, O., & Schwartz, J.E. (1986). Neighborhood and
delinquency: An assessment of contextual effects. Criminology,
24(4), 667-703.

Skinner, B.F. (1953). *Science and human behavior*. New York: Free
Press.

Skinner, B.F. (1969). *Contingencies of reinforcement: A theoretical
analysis*. New York: Appleton-Century-Crofts.

Skinner, B.F. (1974). *About behaviorism*. New York: Vintage Books.

Skinner, W.F., & Fream, A.M. (1997). A social learning theory
analysis of computer crime among college students. Journal of
Research in Crime and Delinquency, 34, 495-518.

Skrondal, A., & Rabe-Hesketh, S. (2004). Generalized latent variable
modeling: Multilevel, longitudinal and structural equation models.
Boca Raton, FL: Chapman & Hall.

Smith, D. (2003). 10 ways practitioners can avoid frequent ethical
pitfalls. Monitor on Psychology, 34(1), 50-55.

Smith, M.D., & Bennett, N. (1985). Poverty, inequality, and theories of
forcible rape. Crime and Delinquency, 31, 295-305.

Smith, M.D., & Brewer, V.E. (1992). A sex-specific analysis of correlates of homicide victimization in United States cities. Violence and Victims, 7, 279-286.

Smith, D.A., & Parker, R.N. (1980). Type of homicide and variation in regional rates. Social Forces, 59, 136-147.

Smith, D.A., & Jarjoura, G.R. (1988). Social structure and criminal victimization. Journal of Research in Crime and Delinquency, 25, 27-52.

Snook, S.C., & Gorsuch, R.L. (1989). Component analysis versus common factor analysis: A Monte Carlo study. Psychological Bulletin, 106, 148-154.

Specht, D.A. (1975). On the evaluation of causal models. Social Science Research, 4, 113-133.

Stafford, M.C., & Ekland-Olson, S. (1982). On social learning and deviant behavior: A reappraisal of the findings: A comment on Akers et al. ASR, August 1979. American Sociological Review, 47(1), 167-169.

Stafford, M.C., & Gibbs, J.P. (1980). Crime rates in an ecological context: Extension of a proposition. Social Science Quarterly, 61, 63-65.

Steffensmeier, D.J., Streifel, C., & Harer, M.D. (1987). Relative cohort size and youth crime in the United States, 1953-1984. American Sociological Review, 52, 702-710.

Steffensmeier, D.J., Streifel, C., & Shihadeh, E.H. (1992). Cohort-size and arrest rates over the life course: The Easterlin hypothesis reconsidered. American Sociological Review, 57, 306-314.

Steffensmeier, D.J., Allan, E.A., Harer, M.D., & Streifel, C. (1989). Age and the distribution of crime. American Journal of Sociology, 94(4), 803-831.

Steiger, J.H. (1990). Structural model evaluation modification: An interval estimation approach. Multivariate Research, 25, 173-180.

Stevens, J. (2002). Applied multivariate statistics for the social sciences (4th ed.). Mahwah, NJ: Lawrence Erlbaum.

Stewart, D.W. (1981). The application and misapplication of factor analysis in marketing research. Journal of Marketing Research, 18, 51-62.

Stone, E.F., & Hollenbeck, J.R. (1984). Some issues associated with the use of moderated regression. Organizational Behavior and Human Performance, 34, 195-213.

Stone, E.F., & Hollenbeck, J.R. (1989). Clarifying some controversial issues surrounding statistical procedures for detecting moderator variables: Empirical evidence and related matters. Journal of Applied Psychology, 74(1), 3-10.

Strickland, D.E. (1982). Social learning and deviant behavior: A specific test of a general theory: A comment and critique. American Sociological Review, 47(1), 162-167.

Sun, I.Y., Triplett, R., & Gainey, R.R. (2004). Neighborhood characteristics and crime: A test of Sampson and Groves' model of social disorganization. Western Criminology Review, 5(1), 1-16.

Sutherland, E.H. (1924). Criminology. Philadelphia: J.B. Lippincott Company.

Sutherland, E.H. (1932). Social process in behavioral problems. Publications of the American Sociological Society, 26, 55-61.

Sutherland, E.H. (1934). Principles of criminology (2nd ed.). Philadelphia: J.B. Lippincott Company.

Sutherland, E.H. (1937). The professional thief. Chicago: University of Chicago Press.

Sutherland, E.H. (1939). Criminology (3rd ed.). Philadelphia: J.B. Lippincott Company.

Sutherland, E.H. (1947). Criminology (4th ed.). Philadelphia: J.B. Lippincott Company.

Sutherland, E.H. (1973a). Development of the theory. In K. Schuessler (Ed.), Edwin H. Sutherland on analyzing crime (pp. 13-29). Chicago: University of Chicago Press.

Sutherland, E.H. (1973b). The person and the situation in the treatment of prisoners. In K. Schuessler (Ed.), Edwin H. Sutherland on analyzing crime (pp. 160-166). Chicago: University of Chicago Press.

Sutherland, E.H. (1973c). Crime and the conflict process. In K. Schuessler (Ed.), Edwin H. Sutherland on analyzing crime (pp. 99-111). Chicago: University of Chicago Press.

Sutherland, E.H. (1973d). Critique of the theory. In K. Schuessler (Ed.), Edwin H. Sutherland on analyzing crime (pp. 30-41). Chicago: University of Chicago Press.

Sutherland, E.H., & Cressey, D.R. (1969). A sociological theory of criminal behavior. In D.R. Cressey & D.A. Ward (Eds.), Delinquency, crime, and social process (pp. 426-432). Albany, NY: State University of New York Press.

Sutherland, E.H., & Cressey, D.R. (1970). Criminology (8th ed.). Philadelphia, PA: J.B. Lippincott Company.

Sutherland, E.H., & Cressey, D.R. (1974). Criminology (9th ed.). Philadelphia, PA: J.B. Lippincott Company.

Sykes, G., & Matza, D. (1957). Techniques of neutralization: A theory of delinquency. American Journal of Sociology, 22, 664-670.

Tabachnick, B.G., & Fidell, L.S. (2001). Using multivariate statistics (4th ed.). Boston: Allyn & Bacon.

Tanaka, J.S. (1987). How big is big enough? Sample size and goodness-of-fit in structural equation models with latent variables. Child Development, 58, 134-146.

Tanaka, J.S., & Huba, G.J. (1989). A general coefficient of determination for covariance structure models under arbitrary GLS estimation. British Journal of Mathematical and Statistical Psychology, 42, 233-239.

Tarde, G. (1912). Penal philosophy (R. Howell, Trans.). Boston: Little Brown.

Thompson, B., & Daniel, L.G. (1996). Factor analytic evidence for the construct validity of scores: A historical overview and some guidelines. Educational and Psychological Measurement, 56(2), 197-208.

Thornberry, T.P. (1987). Toward an interactional theory of delinquency. Criminology, 25, 863-887.

Thornberry, T.P. (1989). Reflections on the advantages and disadvantages of theoretical integration. In S.F. Messner, M.D. Krohn, & A.E. Liska (Eds.), Theoretical integration in the study of deviance and crime (pp. 51-60). Albany, NY: State University of New York Press.

Thornberry, T.P., Lizotte, A.J., Krohn, M.D., Farnworth, M., & Jang, S.J. (1994). Delinquent peers, beliefs, and delinquent behavior: A longitudinal test of interactional theory. Criminology, 32(1), 47-84.

Tinsley, H.E.A., & Tinsley, D.J. (1987). Uses of factor analysis in counseling psychology research. Journal of Counseling Psychology, 34(4), 414-424.

Tittle, C.R. (1985). The assumption that general theories are not possible. In R.F. Meier (Ed.), Theoretical methods in criminology (pp. 93-121). Beverly Hills, CA: Sage.

Tittle, C.R. (1989). Influences on urbanism: A test of three perspectives. Social Problems, 36, 270-288.

Tittle, C.R. (1995). Control balance: Toward a general theory of deviance. Boulder, CO: Westview Press.

U.S. Census Bureau. (1990). United States census 1990 [Data file]. Washington, DC: Available at http://www.census.gov

U.S. Census Bureau. (2000). United States census 2000 [Data file]. Washington, DC: Available at http://www.census.gov

Urberg, K.A. (1992). Locus of peer influence: Social crowd and best friend. Journal of Youth and Adolescence, 21, 439-450.

Urberg, K.A. (1997). Close friend and group influence on adolescent cigarette smoking and alcohol use. Developmental Psychology, 33, 834-844.

Veysey, B.M., & Messner, S.F. (1999). Further testing of social disorganization theory: An elaboration of Sampson and Groves's "community structure and crime." Journal of Research in Crime and Delinquency, 36(2), 156-174.

Vold, G.B. (1958). Theoretical criminology. New York: Oxford University Press.

Voss, H.L. (1964). Differential association and reported delinquent behavior: A replication. Social Problems, 12, 78-85.

Wareham, J., Cochran, J.K., Dembo, R., & Sellers, C.S. (2005). Community, strain, and delinquency: A test of a multi-level model of general strain theory. Western Criminology Review, 6(1), 117-133.

Warner, B.D., & Pierce, G.L. (1993). Reexamining social disorganization theory using calls to the police as a measure of crime. Criminology, 31, 493-517.

Warner, B.D., & Roundtree, P.W. (1997). Local ties in a community and crime model: Questioning the systemic nature of informal social control. Social Problems, 44, 520-536.

Warr, M. (1993). Age, peers, and delinquency. Criminology, 31(1), 17-40.

Warr, M. (1996). Organization and instigation in delinquent groups. Criminology, 34(1), 11-37.

Warr, M. (1998). Life-course transitions and desistance from crime. Criminology, 36, 183-216.

Warr, M. (2002). Companions in crime: The social aspects of criminal conduct. New York: Cambridge University Press.

Webb, S.D. (1972). Crime and the division of labor: Testing a Durkheimian model. American Journal of Sociology, 78, 643-656.

Weicher, J.C. (1970). The effect of income on delinquency: Comment. American Economic Review, 60, 249-256.

Wendorf, C.A. (2002). Comparisons of structural equation modeling and hierarchical linear modeling approaches to couples' data. Structural Equation Modeling, 9(1), 126-140.

West, S.G., Finch, J.F., & Curran, P.J. (1995). Structural equation models with nonnormal variables: Problems and remedies. In R.H. Hoyle (Ed.), Structural equation modeling: Concepts, issues, and applications (pp. 56-75). Thousand Oaks, CA: Sage.

White, H.R., Johnson, V., & Horowitz, V. (1986). An application of three deviance theories for adolescent substance use. International Journal of the Addictions, 21, 347-366.

White, H.R., & LaGrange, R.L. (1987). An assessment of gender effects in self report delinquency. Sociological Focus, 20(3), 195-213.

White, H.R., Pandina, R.J., & LaGrange, R.L. (1987). Longitudinal predictors of serious substance abuse and delinquency. Criminology, 25(3), 715-740.

Wikstrom, P.H., Loeber, R. (2000). Do disadvantaged neighborhoods cause well-adjusted children to become adolescent delinquents? A study of male juvenile serious offending, individual risk and protective factors, and neighborhood context. Criminology, 38(4), 1109-1142.

Williams, K.R. (1984). Economic sources of homicide: Reestimating the effects of poverty and inequality. American Sociological Review, 49, 283-289.

Williams, K.R., & Flewelling, R.L. (1988). The social production of criminal homicide. American Sociological Review, 53, 421-431.

Winfree, L.T., Jr., & Bernat, F.P. (1998). Social learning, self-control, and substance abuse by eighth grade students: A tale of two cities. Journal of Drug Issues, 28(2), 530-558.

Winfree, L.T., Jr., & Griffiths, C.T. (1983). Social learning and adolescent marijuana use: A trend study of deviant behavior in a rural middle school. Rural Sociology, 48(3), 219-239.

Winfree, L.T., Jr., Griffiths, C.T., & Sellers, C.S. (1989). Social learning theory, drug use, and American Indian youths: A cross-cultural test. Justice Quarterly, 6, 395-417.

Winfree, L.T., Jr., Mays, G.L., & Backstrom, T.V. (1994). Youth gangs and incarcerated delinquents: Exploring the ties between gang membership, delinquency, and social learning theory. Justice Quarterly, 11, 229-256.

Winfree, L.T., Jr., Sellers, C.S., & Clason, D.L. (1993). Social learning and adolescent deviance abstention: Toward understanding the reasons for initiating, quitting, and avoiding drugs. Journal of Quantitative Criminology, 9(1), 101-125.

Wirth, L. (1938). Urbanism as a way of life. American Journal of Sociology, 44(1), 1-24.

Wooldredge, J. (2002). Examining the (ir)relevance of aggregation bias for multilevel studies of neighborhoods and crime with an example comparing census tracts to official neighborhoods in Cincinnati. Criminology, 40(3), 681-709.

Zedeck, S. (1971). Problems with the use of "moderator" variables. Psychological Bulletin, 76, 295-310.

Zeger, S.L., & Liang, K.Y. (1986). Longitudinal data analysis for discrete and continuous outcomes. Biometrics, 42, 121-130.

Zhang, L., & Messner, S.F. (2000). The effects of alternative measures of delinquent peers on self-reported delinquency. Journal of Research in Crime and Delinquency, 37(3), 324-337.

Index